To Annette
May God
Bless your
dear one

Letters of
Encouragement

Janeen Stoffregen

TRILOGY CHRISTIAN PUBLISHERS
TUSTIN, CA

Trilogy Christian Publishers
A Wholly Owned Subsidary of Trinity Broadcasting Network
2442 Michelle Drive
Tustin, CA 92780

For information, address Trilogy Christian Publishing

Rights Department, 2442 Michelle Drive, Tustin, Ca 92780.

Trilogy Christian Publishing/ TBN and colophon are trademarks of Trinity Broadcasting Network.

For information about special discounts for bulk purchases, please contact Trilogy Christian Publishing.

Manufactured in the United States of America

Trilogy Disclaimer: The views and content expressed in this book are those of the author and may not necessarily reflect the views and doctrine of Trilogy Christian Publishing or the Trinity Broadcasting Network.

10 9 8 7 6 5 4 3 2 1

Library of Congress Cataloging-in-Publication Data is available.

ISBN 978-1-63769-112-0

ISBN 978-1-63769-113-7 (ebook)

Contents

PART II: Animal Stories and Other Tales

Bossy the Cow and Careless the Crow Series

PART III: Special People & Family Letters and Short Stories

To my dear husband, Bill,
I cherish your love, support, and prayers.
May this encourage you.

Author's Note

Vocal Cord Dysphonia is a neurological disorder that affects your vocal cords, and it's been my constant companion for over twenty-seven years. In struggling with this chronic condition for so long, I believe the Lord used my passion and pain to reach out to others not by oratory grandeur but by sharing God's Word on paper.

I found myself, like Apostle Paul, begging the Lord to take away his thorn in the flesh, and the Lord's response to him became my lifetime verse:

> But he said to me, "My grace is sufficient for you, for my power is made perfect in weakness." Therefore I will boast all the more gladly about my weaknesses, so that Christ's power may rest on me.
>
> 2 Corinthians 12:9 (NIV)

Introduction

The Letters of Encouragement began many years ago, which was prompted by a visit I made to a precious lady in a retirement home. She was only forty-seven years old and was confined to a wheelchair because of severe disabilities from multiple sclerosis.

She had a spunky spirit and confessed she was terribly lonely and felt isolated from everything. I asked what I could do to help, and she quickly responded that she missed getting any personal mail and couldn't use the computer.

I casually mentioned that I was thinking of doing a monthly letter of some kind to help encourage others. I'll never forget her straightforward response. She looked directly at me and smiled. "If you have a gift, use it to help others." Then she boldly added, "Don't think about it, just do it!" I was stunned by her sudden challenge and took it to heart, realizing that letters are personal in an impersonal world.

And so my work began. I soon realized that I had several other friends, and they all had the same thing in common: they were either alone by widowhood, divorce, or were single. Many had health problems and were confined to home, while others were desperately lonely after losing a loved one.

I began the letters by sharing poems, stories, and Scriptures. I also included humor and personal stories and experiences, keeping in mind what my friend had said about feeling isolated and lonely. I wanted the letters to be personal and on pretty paper, and I found myself shopping more for decorator computer paper than for anything else.

Originally, I self-published the letters every month with the help of a local printing company, but I have now combined a special collection of these issues into a book format, which I hope you will enjoy.

In the beginning, the letters went only to a few individuals, but as time passed, they expanded to retirement homes throughout the United States and other places as well, including some schools and a few prisons as well.

No matter how old you are at this stage of the game, I pray these Letters of Encouragement will challenge, inspire and comfort you, no matter what season of life you're in...because you're not alone!

INTRODUCTION

Part I

This special collection of Letters of Encouragement is a unique book for many reasons. This section is an assortment of gripping inspirational stories, poems, and devotional-style messages. They are filled with humor, hope, and pearls of wisdom that I pray will touch your heart.

Part II

This will capture the heart of every animal lover as I shared personal stories about some of our beloved pets. I've also included a satire on marriage with some unusual characters you'll meet named, Bossy the Cow and Careless the Crow. No doubt, they'll make you laugh at their antics of getting along, and who knows, you might even see yourself in these unforgettable barnyard characters.

Part III

This section is about special people, family letters, and my own personal testimony of how God's amazing grace and love changed our life and marriage. In conclusion, I've included some short stories, and I pray these heartfelt messages will be a wonderful way to share your faith with others too.

If you believe God put you here for a purpose,
you will inspire someone.

PART I

Letters of Encouragement

CHAPTER 1

One Day at a Time

In the mornings, while I'm sipping my coffee and reading at the kitchen table, there's a reflection on the wall from the sun behind the window shutters. It's a lovely little design, each with its own little squares filled with sunshine, like a brick painting in shades and shadows.

As I glance at this interesting pattern on the wall, I can't help but think about all the verses in the Bible that tell us to live one day at a time. Yes, indeed! If we can only learn to enjoy today, knowing that our Heavenly Father will see us through whatever comes tomorrow.

One Day at a Time

This is an easy phrase to say,
But not always easy to do.
Thank God, His mercies are new each day,
Giving grace enough to see us through.

We want to know what is out ahead,
But it's best to put our trust in God.
He will see to it we are Spirit-led
As along life's journeys we trod.

It is when we meditate on His Word
We can keep our focus on Him!
For it's by His promises we are assured
He will not leave us out on a limb.

First, we seek His Kingdom and His ways,
And His righteousness above all.
When we do, His joy will brighten our days,
And we know He will answer our call.

Each day has troubles of its own
That is different from the day before.
But God will never leave us alone.
He will take care of our needs and more!

Robbie Mickley

CHAPTER 2

You Are Valued

Many years ago, my husband and I decided to eat dinner at a local restaurant in town. To reach the place, we had to cross a very busy street and used the crosswalk. Right in the middle of the street was a $20 bill, which we stooped down to pick up, thinking for sure it was a fake because it was so badly beaten up.

Surprise, it was real! Apparently, somebody had lost the money, unknowingly. There was no one around to ask if it belonged to them, so we kept it. Even though the bill was dirty and smashed, it was still valuable and worth the same amount, damaged or not.

You Are Valued

A well-known speaker started off his seminar by holding up a $20 bill. In the room of 200, he asked. "Who would like this $20 bill?" Hands started going up. He said, "I am going to give this $20 to one of you—but first, let me do this."

He proceeded to crumple the $20 note up. He then asked. "Who still wants it?" Still, the hands were up in the air. "Well," he replied, "What if I do this?" He dropped it on the ground and started to grind it into the floor with his shoe.

He picked it up, now crumpled and dirty. "Now, who still wants it?" Still, the hands went into the air. "My friends, you have all learned a valuable lesson. No matter what I did to the money, you still wanted it because it did not decrease in value. It was still worth $20."

Many times in our lives, we are dropped, crumpled, and ground into the dirt by the decisions we make and the circumstances that come our way. We feel as though we are worthless, but no matter what happened or what will happen, we will never lose our value.

Unknown Author

Reflection

Take a minute to look back through your experiences in life. See how the Lord has led you through the deserts of life and how He has protected and provided for you. Now consider how He has put up with your complaining and defiant ways, then reflect on how His grace has been enough for all your problems.

After reviewing the past, let your faith expect His future love. The One who has loved and pardoned you will never stop doing so. The more we think about the ways the Lord loves us, let our hearts be on fire to love Him more because of who He is and how He loves us.

CHAPTER 3

Don't Quit

In the beginning, most of the Letters of Encouragement were mailed out monthly. However, there were a few packages that I hand-delivered to some of the local retirement homes. This not only saved me postage but gave me the wonderful opportunity to meet some of the amazing residents and directors of these places over the years.

What a joy it was to meet some of these seniors in various different facilities. Their kind words inspired me to keep doing these letters over the years. I'm grateful for their good attitude, wisdom, and a stellar example of perseverance in not giving up in the difficult seasons of life.

Don't Quit

When things go wrong as they sometimes will,
When the road you're trudging seems all uphill,
When the funds are low and debts are high

And you want to smile, but you have to sigh,
When care is pressing you down a bit,
Rest if you must, but don't you quit.

Life is queer with its twists and turns
As every one of us sometimes learns,
And many a failure turns about
When he might have won had he stuck it out;
Don't give up though the pace seems slow-
You may succeed with another blow.

Success is failure turned inside out-
The silver tint of the cloud of doubt,
And you never can tell how close you are,
It may be near when it seems so far;
So stick to the fight when you're hardest hit-
It's when things seem worse that you must not quit.

John Greenleaf Whittier

CHAPTER 4

A Woman's Poem

They say, "Laughter is the best medicine," so ladies, this one's for you. And let's face it, girls, we can be drama queens when trying to please difficult people, so enjoy these humorous thoughts of retribution.

A Woman's Poem

He didn't like the casserole
And he didn't like my cake,
My biscuits were too hard...
Not like his mother used to make.

I didn't make the coffee right,
He didn't like the stew,
I didn't mend his socks...
The way his mother used to do.

I pondered for an answer
I was looking for a clue.

Then I turned around and smacked him...
Like his mother used to do.

Unknown Author

CHAPTER 5

A Very Special Prayer

As the old saying goes, "You can't judge a book by its cover," and the same is true for people too! It's good to remember that everyone we meet is going through something, and we need to give them as much grace and mercy as God gives us.

A Very Special Prayer

Heavenly Father,

Help us remember that the jerk who cut us off in traffic last night is a single mother who worked nine hours that day and was rushing home to cook dinner, help with homework, do the laundry, and spend a few precious moments with her children.

Help us remember that the pierced, tattooed, disinterested young man who can't make change correctly is a worried nineteen-year-old college student, balancing his apprehension over final exams with the fear of not getting his student loans for the next semester.

Remind us, Lord, that the scary-looking bum, begging for money in the same spot every day (who really ought to get a job), is a slave to addictions that we can only imagine in our worst nightmares.

Help us to remember that the old couple walking annoyingly slow through the store aisles and blocking our shopping progress are savoring this moment, knowing that, based on the biopsy report she got back last week, this will be the last year that they go shopping together.

Heavenly Father, remind us each day that, of all the gifts you give us, the greatest gift is love. It is not enough to share that love with those we hold dear. Open our hearts not just to those who are close to us but to all humanity. Let us be slow to judgment and quick to forgiveness and patience and empathy and love.

Unknown Author

CHAPTER 6

Every Little Bee Counts

A friend of mine related this amazing story of God's grace through a simple act of nature. While swimming in her pool, she saw a bee floating in the water near death. No telling how long the poor little creature had been striving to save its life without success. He was helpless. The water was too deep, and his wings were too wet. The side of the pool was too high, and he was powerless to rescue himself. Death was coming swiftly.

Then quickly, a hand of compassion reached down and saved him from drowning. He lay lifeless on the warm concrete for a while. Suddenly, one wing flipped up, then the other. He fluttered both wings together and flew off into the sunshine, happy to be alive. The little bee had a second chance at life, and now he could go about his life's purpose to pollinate flowers as God purposed for him. Every little bee counts and has a purpose, just like God has a plan for every person.

God saved you by his grace when you believed. And you can't take credit for this; it is
a gift from God. Salvation is not a reward for
the good things we have done, so none of us
can boast about it.

Ephesians 2:89 (NLT)

CHAPTER 7

You're Not Alone

Sometimes words of encouragement come from the most unlikely places, and this one tops the cake. I received a greeting card from an inmate in prison, whom I'd been in contact with for some time.

This amazing man found the Lord in prison, and through the most unusual circumstances, we became acquainted via mail. As time passed, he became my contact point, and the Letters of Encouragement were sent to him, and he, in turn, shared them with others in the facility.

When I received news about his marriage, I was overwhelmed with joy for him. Even though he and his wife couldn't share a life together, he claimed the best part was inheriting an instant family from his wife's children.

After reading his card, I smiled and thought of how good the Lord is to set the lonely ones in families, and remembered this verse which says it all:

"God sets the lonely in families, he leads out the prisoners with singing; but the rebellious live in a sun-scorched land." (Psalm 68:6 NIV)

This was true of my father too. After my mother passed away, Dad lived another seven years with the help of a caregiver. This was a difficult transition, but in time Dad and the caregiver became pals. The caregiver also had other family members in the area, so Dad became part of the package deal. Slowly but surely, my father came out of his shell and became part of another family.

Reflection

Here are a few words I felt the Lord put on my heart to share with the lonely ones like my dad and the man behind bars to remind them they're not alone.

You're Not Alone

I hear your cries of loneliness, but dear heart, I am the God of hope and comfort. I know the deepest need of your soul, which is to know My love. By receiving My Son as your Savior and Lord, you are clean and forgiven. Now you must forgive yourself and others too.

I am calling you in the night. Be still and know that I am God and there is no other. I will never leave or forsake you, for you are Mine. I'm a good Father and will comfort you with My presence and adopt you into My family. Rejoice and be glad, for great is My faithfulness.

CHAPTER 8

All Things Work Together for Good

"And we know that in all things God works for the good of those who love him, who have been called according to his purpose." (Romans 8:28 NIV)

There are times in your life when the people closest to you deeply hurt you, and yet you have to forgive and let the Lord heal your wounds as you move forward.

I was betrayed by a loved one in a financial matter that had long-lasting consequences. When this situation was discovered, I was beside myself with anger and a long list of other raw emotions. In my frustration, I ran out of the house, grabbed my bicycle from the garage, and went for a long ride around the neighborhood.

This always helped me blow off steam by what I call "airing out my brain." I found by getting out in the fresh air it helped release my toxic emotions. With each stride, I peddled harder and faster on my bike with the wind in my face and tears running down.

Once I started to cry, I couldn't stop. I was pouring out my heart to the Lord as I continued to ride my bike with reckless abandon. Then, suddenly I heard the Lord whisper these words in my heart, and I stopped dead in my tracks. "Thank Me for your mistakes because without them you wouldn't be who you are today."

"Oh," I said out loud! Somehow these words were comforting as I rolled them over in my mind. They helped me reconcile the truth of Romans 8:28, which gave me hope to get through this unwanted problem one day at a time.

Yes, I made mistakes; we all do. But the important thing is that God can turn it around when you ask Him to help you. Forgiveness is a choice, and the emotions will catch up later, so take a breath and calm down.

You know you've passed the forgiveness test when the thought of the person, or transgression, comes up, and it's no longer a raw spot. The stinger has been removed!

The deed is not forgotten, but the venom is gone. And by forgiving others, you set yourself free to move forward and enjoy life again.

"Make allowances for each other's faults, and forgive anyone who offends you. Remember, the Lord forgave you, so you must forgive others." (Colossians 3:13 NLT)

CHAPTER 9

Observation on Aging

One of my favorite pastimes is "people watching," and it's even more fun now that I'm an old coot! Yes, "the golden years" may be more brass than gold, but I've learned to keep my chin up, my humor in tacked, and to lighten up.

Observation on Aging

- As you get older, your secrets are safe with your friends. They can't remember them either.
- You can't stay young forever, but you can be immature for your entire life.
- I live in my own little world. But it's okay—they know me there.
- Forget healthy food. I'm at the age where I need all the preservatives I can get.

- I would be unstoppable if I could only get started...
- Aging: Eventually, you will reach a point when you stop lying about your age and start bragging about it.
- The older we get, the fewer things seem worth waiting in line for!
- Some people try to turn back their odometers. Not me! I want people to know why I look this way. I've traveled a long way, and many of the roads weren't paved.
- You know you are getting old when everything either dries up or leaks.
- When you are dissatisfied and would like to go back to your youth, remember Algebra.
- One of the many things no one tells you about aging is that it's better than being young. Being young is beautiful, but being old is comfortable.

Life should not be a journey to the grave with the intention of arriving safely in an attractive and well-preserved body, but rather to skid in sideways, totally worn out and screaming, "Woo-hoo, what a ride!"

Unknown Author

CHAPTER 10

Consider What God Has Done

"Consider what God has done: Who can straighten what He has made crooked." (Ecclesiastes 7:13 NIV)

Have you ever found yourself not understanding God's ways with you? I can definitely say yes to that a hundred times over in my life. However, as one perplexing situation after another ended, I could clearly see God's hand of protection blocking my way, which turned out for my good and His glory.

These pearls of wisdom were only gleaned in hindsight, as you come to trust and believe that God is good and has your best interest at heart, in spite of your fears, doubts, and unbelief at the time.

In the early years of our marriage, I wanted children, but we couldn't have our own. In time, we tried to adopt, but that also failed. The adoption literally was canceled at the eleventh hour, which turned my life upside down.

The "death" of this adoption left me devastated, to say the least. At the time, I was not a Christian, but this life retching event caused me to cry out to God, which forever changed my life and our marriage.

Years later, as I grew in my faith, I came to a profound conclusion that God really did know what was best for me, even though I didn't think so at the time. My plan was not His plan for my life, but He used my gifts, talents, and personality in other ways that suited me better in a working career that lasted for years.

I've often said that God has made worker bees and mother bees, and I'm content to be a worker bee. I also know that when the Lord blocks your plans or takes something away, He always has something better for you...not worst!

"'For I know the plans I have for you,' declares the LORD, 'plans to prosper you and not to harm you, plans to give you hope and a future.'" (Jeremiah 29:11 NIV)

CHAPTER 11

The Pencil Maker

I'm dating myself, but I remember the good old yellow pencils (with a good eraser), and I'm sure you do too. Here are five valuable insights, as shared by a pencil maker before putting the pencils in a box:

The Pencil Maker

1. Everything you do will always leave a mark.
2. You can always correct the mistakes you make.
3. What's important is what is inside you.
4. In life, you will undergo painful sharpening, which will only make you better.
5. To be the best pencil, you must allow yourself to be held and guided by the hand that holds you.

We all need to be constantly sharpened. This parable may encourage you to know that you are a special person with unique God-given talents and abilities.

Only you can fulfill the purpose which you were born to accomplish.

Never allow yourself to get discouraged and think that your life is insignificant and cannot be changed, and, like the pencil, always remember that the most important part of who you are is what's inside you.

Unknown Author

CHAPTER 12

The Missionary and the Lawyer

I recently read a fictional book about a law firm that sent an attorney out to find a woman deep in the jungles of Brazil. She was the sole heir of a large estate. The lawyer finds the woman who is a missionary without any comforts of the modern world. She has dedicated her life to the natives of various jungles tribes and could care less about fame and fortune.

The missionary had no idea she was about to be a very rich woman from her estranged father, now deceased. As the story progresses, she turned down the fortune, and this had such a powerful impact on the attorney that he wanted to know more about her faith in God. As the story continues, she leads the man to faith in Christ after he admits that he has struggled for years with substance abuse and alcoholism.

As the missionary explained to him, it doesn't matter how many times you admit your weakness and failures to counselors; the important thing is to confess it to God. God knows everything anyway, but He won't help unless you ask. God is all-knowing, but you have to go to Him in prayer, in the spirit of humility, and ask for help.

When you do that, your sins will be forgiven. Your slate will be wiped clean, and you will become a new believer in Christ. No matter what difficulty you may be facing, God will give you the strength to deal with it because He is with you!

At this point in the story, the man admitted that he didn't know how to pray, and the missionary asked if she could pray with him. He agreed, and she led him into a simple prayer like this:

Dear God,

Forgive me of my sins and help me forgive others that have done me wrong, and give me strength to overcome my addictions, resentments, and anger toward other people that have hurt me. I need Your help. I no longer can make things work right in my life.

While this is a synopsis of a fictional story, the prayer is real and can be the beginning of the abundant life (knowing Christ) that awaits you...just ask.

"You will pray to him, and he will hear you." (Job 22:27 NIV)

CHAPTER 13

The One Flaw in Women

I'm sure you'll agree that friendships are precious gifts, especially with other women. However, many women fall short in seeing their own value, as you'll see in this uniquely inspiring poem.

The One Flaw in Women

Women have strengths that amaze men...
They bear hardships, and they carry burdens,
but they hold happiness, love, and joy.
They smile when they want to scream.
They sing when they want to cry.
They cry when they are happy
and laugh when they are nervous.
They fight for what they believe in.
They stand up to injustice.
They don't take "no" for an answer
when they believe there is a better solution.

They go without so their family can have.
They go to the doctor with a frightened friend.
They love unconditionally.
They cry when their children excel
and cheer when their friends get awards.
They are happy when they hear about
a birth or a wedding.
Their hearts break when a friend dies.
They grieve at the loss of a family member,
yet they are strong when they
think there is no strength left.
They know that a hug and a kiss
can heal a broken heart.
Women come in all shapes, sizes, and colors.
They'll drive, fly, walk, run or email you
to show how much they care about you.
The heart of a woman is what
makes the world keep turning.
They bring joy, hope, and love.
They have compassion and ideas.
They give moral support to their
family and friends.
Women have vital things to say
and everything to give.
However, if there is one flaw in women,
it is that they forget their worth.

¬Unknown Author

CHAPTER 14

The Measure of a Man

Having children and hanging diplomas on the wall are great achievements, but God looks past our best efforts and values the secret person of the heart. God alone knows the measure of a man, which is the virtuous character that He's forming in you.

The Measure of a Man

Not—How did he die? But—How did he live?
Not—What did he gain? But—What did he give?
These are the things that measure the worth
of a man as a man, regardless of birth.
Not—What was his station? But—had he a heart?
And—How did he play his God-given part?
Was he ever ready with a word of good cheer?
To bring back a smile, to banish a tear?

Not—What was his church? Not—What was his creed?
But—Had he befriended those really in need?
Not—What did the sketch in the newspaper say?
But—How many were sorry when he passed away?
These are the things that measure the worth
of a man, as a man, regardless of birth.

Unknown Author

CHAPTER 15

The Duck and the Devil

Here's a cute story that's an easy read and one you might even relate to as a kid. And just like the children in this story, there's plenty of lessons to learn in life.

The Duck and the Devil

There was a little boy visiting his grandparents on their farm. He was given a slingshot to play with out in the woods. He practiced in the woods, but he could never hit the target. Getting a little discouraged, he headed back for dinner.

As he was walking back, he saw Grandma's pet duck. Just out of impulse, he let the slingshot fly, hit the duck square in the head, and killed it. He was shocked and grieved. In a panic, he hid the dead duck in the woodpile, only to see his sister watching! Sally had seen it all, but she said nothing.

After lunch the next day, Grandma said, "Sally, let's wash the dishes." But Sally said, "Grandma, Johnny told me he wanted to help in the kitchen." Then she whispered to him, "Remember the duck?" So Johnny did the dishes.

Later that day, Grandpa asked if the children wanted to go fishing, and Grandma said, "I'm sorry, but I need Sally to help make supper." Sally just smiled and said, "Well, that's all right because Johnny told me he wanted to help." She whispered again, "Remember the duck?"

So Sally went fishing, and Johnny stayed to help.

After several days doing both his chores and Sally's, he finally couldn't stand it any longer. He came to Grandma and confessed that he had killed the duck. Grandma knelt down, gave him a hug, and said, "Sweetheart, I know. You see, I was standing at the window and I saw the whole thing. But because I love you, I forgave you. I was just wondering how long you would let Sally make a slave of you."

Thought for the day and every day thereafter: Whatever is in your past, whatever you have done—and the devil keeps throwing it up in your face (lying, debt, fear, hatred, anger, unforgiveness, bitterness, etc.) whatever it is, you need to know that God was standing at the window and He saw the whole thing. He has seen your whole life. He wants you to know that He loves you and that you are forgiven. He's just wondering how long you will let the devil make a slave of you.

The great thing about God is that when you ask for forgiveness, He not only forgives you, but He forgets, and it's by God's grace and mercy that we are saved.

Unknown Author

CHAPTER 16

A Simple Hug

In looking back over the years, my most precious gifts were not fancy vacations, expensive jewelry, or luxurious homes, but the love of true friends...and their hugs.

A Simple Hug

There's something in a simple hug
That always warms the heart;
It welcomes us back home
And makes it easier to part.
A hug is a way to share the joy
And sad times we go through,
Or just a way for friends to say
They like you 'cause you're you.
Hugs are meant for anyone
 For whom we really care,
From your grandma to your neighbor,
Or a cuddly teddy bear.

A hug is an amazing thing—
It's just the perfect way
To show the love we're feeling
But can't find the words to say.
It's funny how a little hug
Makes everyone feel good;
In every place and language,
It's always understood.
And hugs don't need new equipment,
Special batteries or parts—
Just open up your arms
And open up your heart.

Unknown Author

CHAPTER 17

God is Faithful

I really like reading the Psalms in the Bible. They are a constant source of encouragement, strength, and hope as we navigate through the difficulties of life. One thing that is a constant theme in the Psalms King David wrote is the transparency of his heart when he cried out to the Lord for help.

King David freely expressed his emotions, fears, and desperate need for help in his prayers (psalms) to the Lord. His prayers became praise! David would end his lament on a positive note, recalling God's lovingkindness and faithfulness, which gave him the confidence to see victory in his present troubles.

David trusted God. He remembered what God had done for him in the past, as he humbly relied on the Lord to give him wisdom and guidance to prevail in the battle at hand.

Again, God's lovingkindness and faithfulness are repeated themes in his psalms. David knew that God was faithful and depended on the Lord, not himself, to save the day.

Although King David didn't write the verses below, it's one of my favorites to remember because it ties in with what David knew in his heart.

I want to encourage you to memorize these few lines. Please remember you can rely on God's faithfulness to see you through, just like Jeremiah did when he penned these words in the Book of Lamentations at a very desperate time in his nation's history and his life.

I recall this to my mind,
Therefore I wait.
The LORD'S acts of mercy indeed do not end,
For His compassions do not fail.
They are new every morning;
Great is your faithfulness.

Lamentations 3:21-23 (NASB)

CHAPTER 18

Inner Peace

Over the years, we've adopted many rescue animals and found our best pets, which have enriched our lives and given us such joy and friendship. Animals give back such unconditional love; it's no wonder why they're called "man's best friend."

Inner Peace Poem

If you can start the day without caffeine or pep pills,
If you can be cheerful, ignoring aches and pains,
If you can resist boring and complaining people with your troubles,
If you can eat the same food every day and be grateful,
If you can understand when loved ones don't give you time,
If you can overlook when people take things out on you,
If you can take criticism and blame without resentment,
If you can face the world without lies and deceit,
If you can conquer tension without medical help,

If you can relax without liquor,
If you can sleep without the aid of drugs,
If you can do all these things
Then you are probably the family dog!

Unknown Author

CHAPTER 19

Reflections

All of us have regrets, make bad decisions, and wrong choices, but that's called being human. The upside of the downside is that we learn from our mistakes.

The wrong way to reflect on our missteps is to brood over them and allow Satan to put a guilt trip on us for sins that we've confessed to the Lord.

A far better way to get "unstuck" is to recall all God has done for us. He is faithful to see us through whatever we are going through. His Word gives us confidence to press on in faith and trust His promises.

Many of us make resolutions around the New Year. For instance: starting a diet, getting more exercise, or whatever the case, but have you ever considered setting some new spiritual goals instead?

For example: Are there any habits, attitudes, or ways of talking that you'd be better off leaving behind? I know for myself, I can be a better listener and not interrupt when someone is talking. Also, I can give more thought to my words before responding to others. Yes, there are lots of areas for improvement...at least for me.

Another area to grow in grace might be to ask the Lord to help us see the best in a contentious person, not the worst. Or how about not overreacting to important decisions before getting all the facts? For me, it's a comforting thought that God doesn't expect perfection... just progress.

So let's leave behind all those bitter thoughts and resentments that can tie us up in knots and keep us from sleeping at night. Instead, let's ask the Lord to help us let go of those things that cause us to stumble, so we can move forward and be pleasing to Him.

> Brothers and sisters, I do not consider myself yet to have taken hold of it. But one thing I do: Forgetting what is behind and straining toward what is ahead, I press on toward the goal to win the prize for which God has called me heavenward in Christ Jesus.
>
> Philippians 3:13-14 (NIV)

CHAPTER 20

The New Top Ten

My husband and I give different ratings to things we've read, like books or movies. When he's done with a book, I always ask where he'd put it on a scale of one to ten. That might be okay for books and movies, but when it comes to encouraging your faith, here's a win-win list.

1. Prayer is not a "spare wheel" that you pull out when you're in trouble, but it's the "steering wheel" that directs the right path breakthrough.

2. Why is a car's windshield so large and the rearview mirror so small? Because our past is not as important as our future. So look ahead and move on.

3. Friendship is like a book. It takes a few seconds to burn but takes years to write.

4. All things in life are temporary. If things are going well, enjoy it because it won't last long. If it's going badly, don't worry, that won't last long either.

5. Old friends are gold. New friends are diamonds! If you get a diamond, don't forget the gold because to hold a diamond, you always need a base of gold.

6. Often when we lose hope and think it's the end, God smiles from above and says, "Relax, sweetheart, it's just a bend, not the end."

7. When God solves your problems, you have faith in His abilities; when God doesn't solve your problems, He has faith in your abilities.

8. A blind person asked St. Anthony, "Can there be anything worse than losing your eyesight?" He replied, "Yes, losing your vision."

9. When you pray for others, God listens to you and blesses them; sometimes, when you're safe and happy, remember that someone has prayed for you.

10. Worrying doesn't take away tomorrow's troubles; it takes away today's peace.

Unknown Author

The Twenty-Third Psalm

One of the most popular Psalms in the Bible is the twenty-third Psalm, with so many good reasons. Consider these thoughts from this Psalm whenever you need reassurance, peace, and comfort from the rich meaning and personal application.

The Twenty-Third Psalm

The LORD is my Shepherd
(That's a relationship, put your name here)

I shall not want
(That's Supply)

He makes me lie down in green pastures
(That's Rest)

He leads me beside the still waters
(That's Refreshment)

He restores my soul
(That's Healing)

He leads me in the paths of righteousness
(That's Guidance)

For His name's sake
(That's Purpose)

Yea, though I walk through the valley of the shadow
of death (That's Testing)

I will fear no evil
(That's Protection)

For You are with me
(That's Faithfulness)

Your rod and Your staff, they comfort me
(That's Discipline)

You prepare a table before me in the presence of my
enemies (That's Hope)

You anoint my head with oil
(That's Concentration)

My cup runs over
(That's Abundance)

Surely goodness and mercy shall follow me all the
days of my life (That's Blessing)

And I will dwell in the house of the LORD
(That's Security)

Forever
(That's Eternity)

Reflection

Are you a lost little lamb that has wandered away
from the flock and gone astray? Even if you are ninety-
five years old and bedridden, He's there for you. When
friends are too busy and family is scarce, He's there for
you. He wants to be more than a religious picture on
your wall; He wants to live in your heart by the power of
the Holy Spirit.

Knowing Him is just a prayer away, "Lord Jesus, I
don't want to live with regret, fear, or guilt as I near the
end of my life. I want to know you as a person, not just

a stained-glass saint on a church window. Come into my heart, forgive my sins and be my Lord, Savior, and friend."

He's waiting for you...just ask!

CHAPTER 22

God's Voice Mail

Don't you hate talking to answering machines instead of real people? With all the modern technology, it's really frustrating to deal with computer-activated devices instead of a "live" person to help you.

Have you ever wondered what it would be like if God decided to install a recording device with a pre-recorded message every time you prayed? Imagine praying and hearing the following options:

God's Voice Mail

Thank you for calling heaven.

For English, press one
For Spanish, press two
For all other languages, press three

Please select one of the following options:

Press one for request
Press two for thanksgiving
Press three for complaints
Press four for all other

I'm sorry, all our angels are helping other customers right now. However, your prayer is important to us, and we will answer it in the order it was received. Please stay on the line. If you would like to speak to:

God, press one
Jesus, press two
Holy Spirit, press three

To find a loved one that has been assigned to heaven, press five and enter their social security number, followed by the pound sign. If you receive a negative response, please hang up and dial area code 666. For reservations to heaven, please enter John 3:16.

For answers to nagging questions about dinosaurs, life, and other planets, please wait until you arrive in heaven for the specifics. Our computers show that you've already been prayed for today.

Please hang up and call again. The office is now closed for the weekend to observe a religious holiday. If you are calling after hours and need emergency assistance, please contact your local pastor.

Thank you, and have a heavenly day.

Unknown Author

CHAPTER 23

God Has Positive Answers

It's really easy to fall into a negative mindset, especially when listening to the news. We are constantly barraged with annoying commercials and mindless TV programs, even with hundreds of channels available.

Then there's all the social media chatter and the constant pressure to be available 24/7. Then we have our own ups and downs of daily life with family, health issues, finances, and the list goes on. Yes, it's easy to get cynical, but God's Word can help us refocus our responses in uncertain times.

For all the downbeat things we say to ourselves, God has positive answers.

You say: "It's impossible."
God says: "All things are possible" (Luke 18:27).

You say: "I'm too tired."
God says: "I will give you rest" (Matthew 11:28).

You say: "Nobody really loves me."
God says: "I love you" (John 3:16 and 13:34).

You say: "I can't go on."
God says: "My grace is sufficient" (11 Corinthians 12:9).

You say: "I can't figure things out."
God says: "I will direct your paths" (Proverbs 3:5-6).

You say: "I can't do it."
God says: "You can do all things through Me" (Philippians 4:13).

You say: "I'm not able."
God says: "I am able" (11 Corinthians 9:8).

You say: "It's not worth it."
God says: "It will be worth it" (Romans 8:28).

You say: "I can't forgive myself."
God says: "I forgive you" (1 John 1:9 and Romans 8:1).

You say: "I can't manage."

God says: "I will supply all your needs" (Philippians 4:19).

You say: "I'm afraid."
God says: "I have not given you a spirit of fear" (11 Timothy 1:7).

You say: "I'm always worried and frustrated."
God says: "Cast all your cares on Me" (1 Peter 5:7).

You say: "I don't have enough faith."
God says: "I've given everyone a measure of faith" (Romans 12:3).

You say: "I feel all alone."
God says: "I will never leave you or forsake you" (Hebrews 13:5).

Keep looking upward!

CHAPTER 24

Suddenly Senior's Creation Story

Many years ago, I was having lunch with my father at one of his favorite places in town. They served great food, and it was always busy with a lively group of seniors from the retirement community.

On the wall was a framed story that was cute and worth and few laughs, so I asked the owner of the restaurant for a copy, and I hope you'll enjoy it too.

Suddenly Senior's Creation Story

On the first day, God created the cow, and God said, "You must go to the field with the farmer all day long, suffer under the sun, have calves, and give milk to support the farmer. I will give you a life span of sixty years." The cow said, "That's a kind of tough life you want me to live for sixty years. Let me have twenty years, and I'll give back the other forty." God agreed.

On the second day, God created the dog. God said, "Sit all day by the door of your house and bark at anyone who comes in or walks past. I will give you a life span of twenty years." The dog said, "That's too long to be barking. Give me ten years, and I'll give back the other ten." So God agreed.

On the third day, God created the monkey. God said, "Entertain people, do monkey tricks, make them laugh. I'll give you a twenty-year life span." The monkey said, "Monkey tricks for twenty years? I don't think so. The dog gave you back ten, so that's what I'll do too, okay?" And God agreed again.

On the fourth day, God created man. God said, "Eat, sleep, play, enjoy. Do nothing, just enjoy, enjoy. I'll give you twenty years." Man said, "What? Only twenty years? No way, man. Tell you what, I'll take my twenty, and the forty the cow gave back, and the ten the dog gave back and the ten the monkey gave back. That makes eighty, okay?" "Okay," said God. "You've got a deal."

So, that's why for the first twenty years, we eat, sleep, play, enjoy and do nothing; for the next forty years, we slave in the sun to support our family; for the next ten years, we do monkey tricks to entertain our grandchildren; and for the last ten years, we sit in the front of the house and bark at everybody.

Unknown Author

CHAPTER 25

Treasures in You

God loves you! He delights in you and has blessed you so that you can be a blessing to others. There are so many simple ways we can show people we care. When God puts someone on your heart, give them a call, send them a note, or better yet, give them a hug whenever possible.

Treasures in You

There are treasures in life, but owners are few
Of money and power to buy things brand new
Yet you can be wealthy and feel regal too,
If you would just look for the treasures in you.

These treasures in life are not hard to find
When you look in your heart, your soul, and your mind.
For when you are willing to share what's within,
Your fervent search for riches will end.

The joy and the laughter, the smile that you bring;
The heart unafraid to love and to sing;
The hand always willing to help those in need;
Ones are quick to reach out, to labor and feed.

So thank you for sharing these great gifts inside;
The caring, the cheering, the hug when one cried.
Thanks for the energy, encouragement too,
And thank you for sharing the treasures in you.

Unknown Author

CHAPTER 26

Each Life Matters to God

As the seasons change, our lives do too—
With so much conflict, you don't know what to do.
What used to be normal is not anymore.
The whole world is affected from shore to shore.

So many are suffering from confusion and loss—
And in these times, we must look to the cross!
It's easy to question, "Why am I here?"
But that just opens the door to doubt and fear.

"Does my life really matter? Is there no other way?"
God answers: "Look unto Me. I'll brighten your day.
To Me, each life matters, for I have a plan
For each boy, girl, woman, and man."

"Though the world is in chaos, I'm still in control.
In the midst of it all, I care for your soul!

Put your trust in Me, take for yourself of my peace—
Cast all your cares upon Me. I'll give you sweet
release."

"I'll fight your battles. You need not be afraid—
The enemy's defeated. Get ready for your victory
parade!"
Yes, our lives matter to God up above—Who sent
His Son Jesus, to show us His love!

Robbie Mickley

CHAPTER 27

Heartprints

Sometimes the best way we can express God's love to others is not by words but by simply leaving an impression on their heart that He is near.

Heartprints

- Whatever our hands touch—we leave fingerprints!
On walls, on furniture, doorknobs, dishes, books—there's no escape!

- As we touch, we leave our identity.

- Oh God, wherever I go today, help me leave heartprints!

- Heartprints of compassion, understanding, and love.

- Heartprints of kindness and genuine concern.

- May my heart touch a lovely neighbor, or a run-away daughter or an anxious mother, or perhaps even a friend.

- Lord, send me out today to leave heartprints.

- And if someone should say, "I felt your touch," May that one sense YOUR LOVE Touching them through ME!

Unknown Author

CHAPTER 28

Reading More and Dancing Less

Our attitude about things can make the difference between enjoying life or merely enduring it. Everyone has problems and difficulties, but this story simplifies the importance of embracing life one day at a time.

Reading More and Dusting Less

I'm reading more and dusting less. I'm sitting in the yard and admiring the view without fussing about the weeds in the garden. I'm spending more time with my family and friends and less time working. Whenever possible, life should be a pattern of experiences to savor, not to endure. I'm trying to recognize these moments now and cherish them.

I'm not 'saving' anything; we use our good china and crystal for every special event such as losing a pound, getting the sink un-stopped, or the first Amaryllis bloom.

I wear my good blazer to the market. My theory is if I look prosperous, I can shell out $28.49 for a small bag of groceries. I'm not saving my good perfume for special parties but for wearing it for clerks in the hardware store and tellers at the bank.

"Someday" and "one of these days" are losing their grip on my vocabulary. If it's worth seeing, hearing, or doing, I want to do it now. I'm not sure what others would have done had they know they wouldn't be here for the "tomorrow" that we all take for granted. I think they would have called family members and a few close friends to apologize and mend fences for past squabbles.

I like to think they would have gone out for a Chinese dinner or for whatever their favorite food was. I'm guessing; I'll never know. It's those little things left undone that would make me angry if I knew my hours were limited.

Angry because I hadn't written certain letters that I intended to write one of these days. Angry and sorry that I didn't tell my husband and parents often enough how much I truly love them.

I'm trying very hard not to hold back or save anything that would add laughter and luster to the lives of others. And each morning when I open my eyes, I tell myself that it is special. Every day, every minute, every breath truly is a gift from God.

Ann Wells

CHAPTER 29

The Holy Alphabet

Have you ever considered reciting the alphabet when you can't sleep? Probably not, but this little poem reminds us to calm down, refocus, and keep looking up to the One who can help us.

The Holy Alphabet

A-Although things are not perfect
B-Because of trial or pain
C-Continue in thanksgiving
D-Do not begin to blame
E-Even when the times are hard
F-Fierce winds are bound to blow
G-God is forever able
H-Hold on to what you know
I-Imagine life without His love
J-Joy would cease to be
K-Keep on thanking Him for all the things
L-Love imparts to thee

M-Move out of "Camp Complaining"

N-No weapon that is known

O-On earth can yield the power

P-Praise can do alone

Q-Quit looking at the future

R-Redeem the time at hand

S-Start every day with worship

T-To "thank" is a command

U-Until we see Him coming

V-Victory in the sky

W-We'll run the race with gratitude

X-Xalting God most high

Y-Yes, there'll be good times and some bad, but...

Z-Zion waits in glory...where none are ever sad!

Unknown Author

CHAPTER 30

The Butterfly

There are so many little creatures that come to life in the springtime, but my favorite has always been watching the transformation of the caterpillar into a butterfly. To witness these poor creatures' struggle and then to see them freed of the shell is truly amazing to behold.

The Butterfly

A man was walking one morning in the park and came across the cocoon of a butterfly. He sat down on a bench under the tree and was fascinated by the unveiling of the little creature. He watched for a long time with excitement as part of the butterfly was out but then became distressed because it struggled so hard to break through the small opening in the cocoon.

Then the butterfly stopped making any progress! It looked as if the battle was hopeless, and the poor little thing was unable to get out any further. At this time, the man couldn't stand to see it suffer anymore and decided to help. In his own wisdom, he took a pair of scissors and snipped off the remaining bit of the shell, and the butterfly finally emerged easily, but it had a swollen body and small, shriveled wings.

The man then continued to watch the butterfly and expected that, at any moment, the wings would enlarge and expand, and it would be able to support its body and fly away. What the man in his kindness and haste did not understand was that the restriction to get out of the cocoon was God's way of helping the little creature.

When the butterfly strained to get out of the small opening, it forced fluid from its body to the wings, which then made it ready for flight once free from the shell.

Sometimes struggles are exactly what we need in our lives. If God allowed us to go through life without any obstacles, it would cripple us, and we would not see the results of answered prayer and know God in a personal and powerful way. God has promised to provide for our needs, not our greed, as we learn to trust Him, believe in Him, and rest in His promises.

Unknown Author

CHAPTER 31

The Onion

I don't know how you feel about raw onions, but I dislike them immensely. For me, it's a childhood hatred because I was forced (strongly urged by my parents) to eat something with onions in it. That was it, and to this day, I will not eat anything with raw onions. However, I use them when cooking, and especially like them in homemade soups, but the keyword here is cooked before they pass my lips.

The Onion

I was an onion before Christ set me free.
Layers upon layers of iniquity.
An ugly old onion that's fragrance was strong:
That my Jesus bought and loved all along.

Unknown to me what He was going to do.
Of what He was planning, I had not a clue.
Pulling each layer off one by one.
In order to make me more like Jesus the Son.

The first layer wasn't so bad.
I saw all the sins I knew I had.
They were easy to fix, just change the way I talk.
And learn more of how He wanted me to walk.

Reading His Word and learning again;
How to put aside my life of sin.
But the next layer was pulled, which hurt more.
He was getting closer to the core.

Unknown what He would find there.
I simply gave it to Him in prayer.
As another layer was removed, He started to cry;
Pulling this layer brought pain to my Father on High.

And I was crying over the sadness I felt;
The brokenness and all of the guilt.
Past memories that I thought were gone;
They were buried under layers disguised in a fragrance so strong.

As onions peel more and more;
And put tears in our eyes as we get close to the core;
So my Father wept over my pain;
Giving me a balm of comfort and strength to sustain.

No more layers, "I would scream.
As He continued to peel them off of me.

I'll have nothing left, my Lord; what will I do?
I'll be nothing but a worthless core to you."

But He said, "Trust me," and continued to peel.
I was sure He was blinded to my pain that was so
real.
Year after year, I shrunk more and more; Until all
that was left was a core.

It was then that I began to understand;
As the Lord embraced me in His loving hand.
He said, now and only now can you be;
The creation that will minister before Me.

Clothed with the righteousness only from above;
Gone are your layers of self so you can be filled with
My love.
He took my layers of sin, hurt, and pain;
And clothed me with love, truth, and mercy in His
name.

Yes, we are all onions learning each day;
How to overcome as each layer is taken away.
Some layers tear and pull at our heart.
While others grieve us to our innermost part.

But we are nothing but an ugly onion without Christ.
Layers upon layers of pride, sin, and strife.

Only God can take those layers away.
And clothe us with His righteousness in that final
day.

Unknown Author

CHAPTER 32

Wisdom Nuggets: Volume 1

Many years ago, I jotted down little power points in the back of my Bible, which are just as meaningful today as they were years ago when I scribbled them down. I lovingly call these next four chapters the "Wisdom Nuggets."

- Nobody accidentally goes to heaven—you need to make a choice.
- Make your plans so big, you know you'll fail without God.
- God is the sender, the Holy Spirit is the quickener, and Christ is the revealer.
- Just because you can't see air, don't stop breathing. Just because you can't see God, don't stop believing!
- Knowing "it" isn't enough; you have to know Him.

- It's easier to save us from our sins than from our own sense of righteousness.
- To "obey" simply means to follow.
- Love in action: Jesus in you!
- Have confidence in God, not yourself.
- If you're all wrapped up in yourself, you're a pretty small package.
- Faith means embracing Jesus alone.
- The abundant life is intimacy with Jesus.
- If you open your heart to the Lord, He will open Heaven to you.
- When fear knocks at your door—let faith answer it.
- Jesus died so that you can be forgiven, fruitful and fulfilled.
- God forgives and forgets—let's do the same with each other.
- The more Godly you become, the more merciful you are.
- If you take care of God's business, He'll take care of you.
- The man who kneels to God can stand up to anything.
- God never takes something away from you unless He gives you something better.
- Live under the smile of God—it's His nature to bless.

- Don't focus on what He's not doing, but only who He is.
- God's job is to protect and provide for us; our job is to trust and believe.
- When you feel you don't have to earn God's favor, you're free!
- God loves you, and Jesus died for you!
- Conscience is not the voice of God but the gift of God.
- When you know the faithfulness of God, you don't have to fear anything.
- Jesus was God with skin on.
- The God of the Bible is a Person, not a religion.
- Your security in Jesus is the anchor of your soul.
- The harder the conflict, the more glorious the triumph.
- Encouragement from God is like oxygen to the soul.
- Fear turned into prayer becomes courage.
- The Gospel means you can stop trying to please God by your own efforts.
- If a dying Savior can save us, then a living Savior can certainly, keep us.
- He forgives our sins but remembers our weakness.
- God doesn't grade on the curve; He died for the whole world.

- The greater the trial—the greater the grace.
- I'm living with Jesus 'cause He's in my heart.
- I will not fear the battle if You are by my side.
- Prayer is a handclasp with God.
- Kindness refreshes the hearts of God's people.

CHAPTER 33

Wisdom Nuggets: Volume 2

- Kind words are music to broken hearts.
- Past failures are guideposts for future success.
- Happiness is like jam...you can't spread even a little without getting some on yourself.
- If you want to touch God's heart, use the name He loves to hear, call Him Father.
- Greatness is not measured by how many servants you have, but by how many people you serve.
- What God promises, He will provide!
- The reason a dog has so many friends is that he wags his tail instead of his tongue.
- Two things are hard on the heart; running upstairs and running down people.
- To forgive is to set a prisoner free and discover the prisoner was you!
- Jesus is a friend who walks in when the world has walked out.

- Faith is remembering I am God's priceless treasure, when I feel utterly worthless.
- Fear not tomorrow, for God is already there...
- Man never discloses his own character so clearly, as when he describes another's.
- The best way to face life's changes is to look to the unchanging God.
- You can't claim God as your Father until Jesus is your Savior.
- God's throne is mercy, not marble.
- A person filled with joy preaches without preaching, and a day hemmed in prayer seldom unravels.

CHAPTER 34

Wisdom Nuggets: Volume 3

- Many folks want to serve God, but only as advisers.
- It's easier to preach ten sermons than to live one.
- The Good Lord didn't create anything without a purpose, but mosquitoes come close.
- Opportunity may knock once, but temptation bangs at your front door forever.
- The phrase that is guaranteed to wake up an audience is "and in conclusion."
- To make a long story short, don't tell it.
- Some minds are like concrete: thoroughly mixed up and permanently set.
- Peace starts with a smile.
- Faith is believing what God has already said.
- If you have a Bible, read it and let God speak to you.
- God promises a safe landing, not a calm passage.

- People are funny. They want the front of the bus, the middle of the road, and the back of the church.
- God knows your name and feels your pain.
- If God is your co-pilot, swap seats!
- He who angers you controls you.
- The will of God will never take you to where the grace of God will not sustain you.
- Kindness is difficult to give away because it keeps coming back.
- Forgiveness is the ultimate freedom.

CHAPTER 35

Wisdom Nuggets: Volume 4

- God never called us to be successful, just faithful.
- In God's presence, we don't have to be brave.
- Waiting on God is an exercise in patience and obedience.
- To be in Christ is a creative adventure.
- Money is a tool, not a measure of our worth.
- Don't judge Christ by those who imperfectly bear His name.
- God will bless the work of our hands, provided they are not in our pocket.
- Finding God is not a group activity; it's an individual pursuit.
- Backbones are better than wishbones, but "faith bones" are the best.
- Faith that has not been tested cannot be trusted.
- Who I am is more valuable than what I have.

- Christianity is Christ. He is a person, not a religion.
- Life is God's gift to you. What you do with it is your gift to Him.
- If you're thankful, you'll be peaceful.
- Pray about everything, and don't worry about anything.
- Prayer is the slender nerve between myself and the arm of God.
- The Gospel is God's message, not a Christian opinion.
- If you think lightly of your sin, you think lightly of your Savior.
- You'll never know Jesus is all you need until Jesus is all you have.
- God may not give you all your expectations, but He will give you His promises.
- Praying is simply talking to God.
- A church alive is worth the drive.
- Fear is the wrong answer to using your imagination.
- Sometimes, the storms of life still rage, but God will calm the heart of His child.
- Being steadfast means that you have settled it in your mind that God will take care of you.
- You can never be too bad to be saved, but you can be too late.

- Through the darkest night, His light will shine bright.
- Forgiveness of sins is the jewel of the Gospel.

CHAPTER 36

Be Still and Know

I'm sure we all experience people that call us and end up doing all the talking. My husband calls this "having a listening experience" and just nods and doesn't get a chance to say much. God bless him for his patience!

Sometimes that's how it is with our prayers too. Many times we're so busy talking, giving the Lord our laundry list, we forget to be still and let His thoughts and words speak to our heart by being still.

Be Still and Know

Time seems to pass more quickly
Each year that hurries by.
It's no longer "slow and laid back,"
But has donned wings and seems to fly.

With knowledge increasing daily,
Technology adds speed to its pace.
Life zooms by before you know it,
And we find ourselves in a rat race.

For those of us who are God's children,
We're not to keep up the world's pace.
God calls us to "be still and KNOW Him,"
We're to dwell in His secret place!

We need to take time to fellowship
With this God who loves us so much!
From His Word and His still small voice,
We are restored by His loving touch.

We come to understand Who He is and
Just how much He really cares.
In His presence, we learn to trust Him
With all our burden and cares.

So stop running the rat race and be still!
Get to know Him as never before.
Life will be so much more meaningful as you
Get to know Him more and more.

Robbie Mickley

CHAPTER 37

Joy is Knowing

It's fun to use the Thesaurus because you can gleam other word choices for something you want to describe without overuse of the same word.

For instance, when you look at the word joy, there are quite a few selections like delight, pleasure, gladness, happiness, and so forth.

My challenge to you is, what's your definition of joy? For me, this precious little word is power-packed with meaning. I guess I might describe it as having a calm delight, knowing that Lord is with me.

I was going through some old journal notes (written many years ago) when I was going through an extremely stressful season of life helping my father after my mother died. Here are some of the things I wrote about joy in the midst of these troublesome times.

Joy is Knowing

The joy of the Lord is knowing He is in control of every problem and circumstance. The joy of the Lord is having His calm assurance that when fiery trials come, they will also go.

The joy of the Lord is knowing that He loves you and keeps you in all your ways. He looks down from Heaven and sees hearts, not people. Hearts that look to Him for help, forgiveness, and mercy. He gives His power and Spirit to those who wait for Him to work on their behalf. He looks for those who want to do the right things and honor Him.

God looks for those to share His love with in an unbelieving and evil world that has turned away from His Word, His love, and His Son. He gives hope and joy to those who seek His face and those who call on His name and follow Him and walk in His ways.

The joy of the Lord is knowing He is there for all seasons—and He lives to make intercession for those who love Him and are called according to His purposes.

The joy of the Lord is knowing the best is yet to come. God is greater than all my hopes and stronger than all my fears. I am not afraid. My God will help me walk through these difficult days and show me His strength in my weakness and His hope in my despair. His joy, for my sorrow!

Reflection

At the time I wrote these thoughts, I was overwhelmed with family challenges, but thankfully, they are all resolved. So, I want to encourage you not to get stuck on your feelings and negative emotions but pour out your heart to the Lord. He hears, He cares, and He knows the daily struggles we face. Let your faith rise up and be stronger than your fears.

"In Him our hearts rejoice, for we trust in his holy name" (Psalm 33:21 NIV).

CHAPTER 38

When I Got to Heaven

There are lots of jokes about Heaven, but this clever little poem says it best. No doubt, every saint has a past, and every sinner has a future...and a few surprises too.

When I Got to Heaven

I was shocked, confused, bewildered
As I entered Heaven's door
Not by the beauty of it all
By the lights or its décor.

But it was the folks in Heaven
Who made me sputter and gasp
The thieves, the liars, the sinners
The alcoholics, the trash.

There stood the kid from seventh grade
Who swiped my lunch money twice
Next to him was my old neighbor
Who never said anything nice.

Uncle Bill, who I always thought
Was rotting away in hell
Was sitting pretty on cloud nine,
Looking terribly well.

I nudged Jesus, "What's the deal?
I would love to hear Your take
How'd all these sinners get up here?
God must've made a mistake."

"And why is everyone so quiet
So somber? Please give me a clue."
"Hush, child," He said, "They're all in shock
No one thought they'd be seeing you!"

Unknown Author

CHAPTER 39

The Gold and Black Box

One year my husband and I had an unusual weekend of attending two lifetime events. One was a funeral, and the other was a wedding. As you can imagine, these two events couldn't be more diverse by way of celebration, just like this poem about the gold and black box.

The Gold and Black Box

I have in my hands two boxes.
Which God gave me to hold.
He said, "Put all your sorrows in the black box,
And all your joys in the gold."

I heeded His words and in the two boxes,
Both my joys and sorrows I stored,
But though the gold became heavier each day,
The black was light as before.

With curiosity, I opened the black,
I wanted to find out why,
 And I saw, in the base of the box, a hole,
Which my sorrows had fallen out by.

I showed the hole to God and mused,
"I wonder where my sorrows could be!"
He smiled a gentle smile and said,
"My child, they're all here with me."

I asked God why He gave me the boxes,
Why the gold and the black with the hole?
"My child, the gold is for you to count your blessings,
 The black is for you to let go."

Unknown Author

CHAPTER 40

Don't Worry

Years ago, I was enthralled as I listened to a pastor who for several years had faithfully served the church. His executive responsibilities had taken him all over this country. As he concluded his message, he told of one of the most frightening yet thought-provoking experiences of this life.

He had been on a long flight from one place to another. The first warning of the approaching problems came when the sign on the airplane flashed on: "Fasten your seat belts." Then, after a while, a calm voice said, "We shall not be serving the beverages at this time as we are experiencing some turbulence. Please be sure your seat belt is fastened."

As he looked around the aircraft, it became obvious that many of the passengers were becoming apprehensive. Later, the voice of the announcer said, "We are so sorry that we are unable to serve the meal at this time. The turbulence is still ahead of us." Then the storm broke.

The ominous cracks of thunder could be heard even above the roar of the engines. Lightning lit up the darkening skies, and within moments that great plane was like a cork tossed around on a celestial ocean. One moment the airplane was lifted on terrific currents of air; the next, it dropped as if it were about to crash. The pastor confessed that he shared the discomfort and fear of those around him.

He said, "As I looked around the plane, I could see that nearly all the passengers were upset and alarmed. Some were praying. The future seemed ominous, and many were wondering if they would make it through the storm."

Then, suddenly, I saw a little girl. Apparently, the storm meant nothing to her. She had tucked her feet beneath her as she sat on her seat; she was reading a book and everything within her small world was calm and orderly. Sometimes she closed her eyes, then she would read again; then she straightened her legs, but worry and fear were not in her world.

When the plane was buffeted by the terrible storm and rose and fell with frightening severity, all the adults were scared half to death, but that marvelous child was completely composed and unafraid. The minister could hardly believe his eyes.

It was not surprising, therefore, that when the plane finally reached its destination, and all the passengers were hurrying to disembark, our pastor lingered to speak to the girl whom he had watched for a long time. Having commented about the storm and the behavior of the plane, he asked why she had not been afraid.

The child replied, "Cause my daddy's the pilot, and he's taking me home."

There are many kinds of storms that buffet us:

Physical, mental, financial, domestic, and...many other storms that can easily and quickly darken our skies and throw our plane into apparently uncontrollable movement.

We have all know such times, and let us be honest and confess, it is much easier to be at rest when our feet are on the ground than when we are being tossed about a darkened sky.

Let us remember...Our Father is the pilot. He is in control and taking us home...so don't worry.

Unknown Author

CHAPTER 41

Rules for Dieting

For all of us who have tried to lose a few pounds, we all know there's a multitude of diets to choose from, but here's a few rules that everyone should love.

Rules for Dieting

- If you eat something and no one sees you eat it, it has no calories.
- If you drink diet soda with candy bars, the calories in the candy bar are canceled out by the diet soda.
- When you eat with someone else, calories don't count as long as you don't eat more than they do.
- Food used for medicinal purposes never counts, such as hot chocolate, toast, and Sara Lee cheesecake.
- If you fatten up the people around you, then you look thinner.

- Movie-related foods do not have additional calories because they are part of the entire entertainment package and are not part of one's personal intake. Examples are Milk Duds, buttered popcorn, Junior Mints, Red Hots, and Tootsie Rolls.
- Cookie pieces contain no calories. The process of breaking cookies causes caloric leakage.
- Things licked off knives and spoons have no calories if you are in the process of preparing something. Examples are peanut butter on a knife while making a sandwich or ice cream on a spoon while making a sundae.
- Foods that have the same color have the same number of calories. For instance, spinach and pistachio ice cream, cauliflower and whipped cream. Note: Chocolate is a universal substitute and may be used in place of any other food.

Unknown Author

CHAPTER 42

The Mayo Jar and Two Cups of Coffee

A professor stood before his philosophy class and had some items in front of him. When the class began, without a word, he picked up a very large and empty mayonnaise jar and proceeded to fill it with golf balls. Then he asked the students if the jar was full. They agreed it was.

The professor then picked up a box of pebbles and poured them into the jar. He shook the jar lightly, and the pebbles rolled into the open areas between the golf balls. Then he asked the students again if the jar was full. They agreed it was. The professor then picked up a box of sand and poured it into the jar. Of course, the sand filled up everything else. He asked once more if the jar was full. The students responded with a unanimous "yes."

The professor then produced two cups of coffee from under the table and poured the entire contents into the jar, effectively filling the empty space between the sand. The students laughed. "Now," said the professor, as the laughter subsided, "I want you to recognize that this jar represents your life. The golf balls are the important things—your faith in God, your family, your children, your health, your friends, and your favorite hobbies. Things that if everything else was lost and only they remained, your life would still be full."

"The pebbles are the other things that matter like your job, your house, and your car. The sand is everything else-all the small stuff."

"If you put the sand into the jar first," he continued, "there is no room for the pebbles or the golf balls. The same goes for life. If you spend all your time and energy on the small stuff, you will never have room for the things that are important to you.

"Pay attention to the things that are critical to your happiness. Play with your children. Take time to get medical checkups. Take your partner out to dinner. Play another eighteen holes of golf. There will always be time to clean the house and fix the disposal.

"Take care of the golf balls first, the things that really matter. Set your priorities. The rest is just sand."

One of the students raised her hand and asked what the coffee represented. The professor smiled. "I'm glad you asked. It goes to show you that no matter how full your life may be, there's always room for coffee with a friend."

Unknown Author

CHAPTER 43

God Knows Your Sorrows

Just as the weather can suddenly change, so can our lives with just one phone call. We can get bad news about our health, a family problem, or are suddenly facing a financial crisis. We may feel helpless and afraid as we go through these storms of life...but we are not alone!

God Knows Your Sorrows

Are you going through a great difficulty?
Have wrong choices made your sorrow deep?
Does each moment become so heavy,
That much of the time you weep?

It's not only you—there are others
Who suffer this same kind of pain.
Yet, under the eye of your Father,
Your prayers will not be in vain.

When it seems the worst has happened,
Yet, your heart continues to break.
Hold tight to the hand of your Father–
For He knows how much you can take.

God is always working,
Though outward, nothing seems to change.
It takes time for wills to be broken,
So lives may be rearranged.

Leave them in the hands of your Father,
Though this is not easy to do.
Take one day at a time, and trust Him,
He's also concerned about you.

Rest assured, others are praying,
They are there to help you bear
Your burdens for your loved ones,
To the Father's throne in prayer.

Remember, Praise is important—
It keeps hope alive in your soul.
What seems impossibly broken,
God will delight in making whole.

Robbie Mickley

CHAPTER 44

Noah's Ark

It's always good to learn new things, so in keeping with the theme of a teachable spirit, here are some valuable lessons learned by taking a voyage of Biblical proportion.

Noah's Ark: Everything I need to know, I learned from Noah's Ark.

One:	Don't miss the boat.
Two:	Remember that we're all in the same boat.
Three:	Plan ahead. It wasn't raining when Noah built the Ark.
Four:	Stay fit. When you're sixty years old, someone may ask you to do something really big.
Five:	Don't listen to the critics; just get on with the job that needs to be done.

Six: Build your future on high ground.

Seven: For safety's sake, travel in pairs.

Eight: Speed isn't always an advantage. The snails were on board with the cheetahs.

Nine: When you're stressed, float awhile.

Ten: Remember, the Ark was built by amateurs; the Titanic by professionals.

Eleven: No matter the storm, when you're with God, there's always a rainbow waiting.

Unknown Author

CHAPTER 45

My Life is but a Tapestry

Our life is like a beautiful tapestry, an ongoing work in progress, just like this poem expresses with the light and dark threads of life that we all experience.

My Life is but a Tapestry

My life is but a weaving
Between the Lord and me;
I cannot choose the colors,
He works so steadily.

Oft times He weaves in sorrow,
And I in foolish pride,
Forget He sees the upper
And I the underside.

Not until the loom is silent
And the shuffles cease to fly
Will God unroll the tapestry
And explain why.

The dark threads are as needed
In the Weaver's skillful hand,
As the threads of gold and silver
In the pattern He has planned.

He knows, He loves, He cares,
Nothing this truth can dim.
He gives His very best to those
Who leave the choice with Him.

Unknown Author

CHAPTER 46

Remember When?

My best friend has a "Remember When" page in the back of her Bible. She told me it was her bragging book about God and reminded her of God's faithfulness in the past. By doing so, it gave her confidence in God's promises to help her again when future problems arise.

How about you? Do you have a list of things that the Lord has seen you through? I do, and I like to remember how the Lord has sustained, healed, and provided for us in some very difficult times.

I recall when: My husband survived a near-fatal car accident and fully recovered. The Lord miraculously saved him and spared me because I was not with him.

I recall when: I fell at a neighbor's house and shattered my knee cap, broke my wrist, and sprained my other ankle. I healed beautifully without surgery, and my job was waiting for me when I was able to return.

I recall when: After my mother passed, I helped my dad for seven years, and with the help of a caregiver, he was able to stay in his home.

I recall when: My husband, over the span of a few years, had two mild strokes, and fortunately, he had only minor setbacks and was able to work again.

I recall when: We had to sell our home toward the end of the great financial meltdown in 2010. At the same time, my husband was diagnosed with colon cancer. We found another home that we loved even more, and he's been cancer-free for years!

Everyone has difficulties we go through, and I don't know about you, but seeing these events from hindsight, encourages my faith in the future. After living through these things, I can clearly see how the Lord provided, healed, and sustained us during these terrible situations, and He will do the same for you!

CHAPTER 47

The Fern and the Bamboo

Have you ever had days you just wanted to quit? We all do at times, which is why it's easy to relate to this story about the fern and the bamboo. It's a good reminder to not give up and remember how patient God is with us.

The Fern and the Bamboo

One day I decided to quit...I quit my job, my relationship, my spirituality. I wanted to quit my life. I went to the woods to have one last talk with God.

"God," I said, "Can you give me one good reason not to quit?" His answer surprised me. "Look around," He said. "Do you see the fern and the bamboo?" "Yes," I replied.

"When I planted the fern and the bamboo seeds, I took very good care of them. I gave them light. I gave them water. The fern quickly grew from the earth, and its brilliant green covered the floor. Yet nothing came from the bamboo seed. But I did not quit on the bamboo.

"In the second year, the fern grew more vibrant and plentiful. And again, nothing came from the bamboo seed. But I did not quit on the bamboo.

"In the third year, there was still nothing from the bamboo seed. But I would not quit. In the fourth year, again, there was nothing from the bamboo seed. But I would not quit.

"Then, in the fifth year, a tiny sprout emerged from the earth. Compared to the fern, it was seemingly small and insignificant. But just six months later, the bamboo rose to over 100 feet tall. It had spent the five years growing roots. Those roots made it strong and gave it what it needed to survive. I would not give any of my creations a challenge it could not handle.

"Did you know, my child, that all this time you have been struggling, you have actually been growing roots? I would not quit on the bamboo; I will never quit on you! Don't compare yourself to others." He said, "The bamboo had a different purpose than the fern. Yet, they both make the forest beautiful. Your time will come," God said to me.

"You will rise high!" "How high should I rise?" I asked. "How high will the bamboo rise?" He asked in return. "As high as it can?" I questioned. "Yes," He said, "Give Me glory by rising as high as you can." I left the forest, realizing that God will never give up on me. And He will never give up on you. Never regret a day of your life. Good days give you happiness; bad days give you experiences; both are essential to life.

Unknown Author

CHAPTER 48

Blue Hair is Cool

It's often been said that aging is not for sissies. Can I get an "Amen" out there? As we deal with all kinds of aches and pains, it helps to keep our sense of humor in tacked, and our appearance as well...including the color of our hair.

I can't help but smile when I think about my grandmother. You guessed it! She had blue hair more times than not.

She and my grandfather had an apartment in town, and I use to visit them often as a teenager. Many times after high school, I would stop by and see grandma teasing her beautiful hair, but sometimes she left the color on too long, and it turned blue.

When this happened, she shrugged her shoulders and said, "Oh, well, blue is a cool color." My grandma was a real shaker and mover. When she was in her seventies, she obtained her real estate license; when she turned eighty, she and grandpa went to Hawaii on a cruise ship. She took hula lessons and had fun on the trip, even though grandpa couldn't do much.

My grandfather had a stroke years before, which affected his speech, and he had crippled hands—however, he still had fairly good mobility, but nothing compared to grandma. Needless to say, she was an inspiration and very attractive at her age.

When grandma passed away, my parents said it was a peaceful transition into the arms of her beloved Lord. What I admired most about her was her adventurous spirit and inner strength. She lived big and loved much. She was the real deal and lived the life of faith without preaching a word.

I also remember a green marble she cherished in a keepsake little blue velvet box. It had a gold band around the stone with an inscription about the Golden Rule in the Bible. I'll always remember this marble, and the kind of life my grandma lived...and the legacy of faith she left behind.

"Do to others whatever you would like them to do to you. This is the essence of all that is taught in the Law and the prophets." (Matthew 7:12 NLT)

CHAPTER 49

Hands

If our hands could talk, they would certainly tell a lot about our life, just like this story about an old man and a stranger that met one day in the park. Little did the stranger know that this man and their conversation would never be forgotten or how he viewed his hands again.

Hands

I noticed an old man, some ninety-plus years, sitting feebly on the park bench as I sat down to rest. He didn't move. He just sat there with his head down, staring at his hands. When I sat down, he didn't notice me or say a word. Finally, not wanting to disturb him but wanting to be sure he was okay, I asked if he was alright.

He raised his head and looked at me and smiled. "Yes, I'm fine. Thank you for asking," he said in a clear, strong voice. "I didn't want to bother you, but you were just sitting there staring at your hands, and I wanted to check to see if you were okay," I explained.

"Have you ever looked at your hands?" He asked. "I mean, really looked at your hands?" I slowly opened up my hands and stared down at them. I turned them over, palms up and then palms down, "No, not really," I said as I tried to figure out the point he was making.

Then he smiled and related this story: "Stop and think a moment about your hands, and how they have served you well throughout your years. These hands, though wrinkled, shriveled, and weak, have been the tools I have used all my life to reach out and grab and embrace life.

"They supported and caught my fall when I was a toddler and crashed upon the floor. They put food in my mouth and clothes on my back. As a child, my mother taught me to fold them in prayer. They tied my shoes and pulled on my boots. They dried the tears of my children and caressed my wife. They held my rifle and wiped my tears when I went off to war.

"They have been dirty, scraped, and raw. They were decorated with my wedding band to show the world I was married and loved someone special. My hands were uneasy and clumsy when I tried to hold my newborn son.

"They wrote letters home and trembled and shook when I buried my parents and wife and walked my daughter down the aisle. Yet, they were strong and sure when I dug my buddy out of a foxhole and lifted a plow off my best friend's foot.

"They have held children, consoled neighbors, and shook in fists of anger when I didn't understand. They have covered my face, combed my hair, and washed and cleansed my body. And to this day, not much of anything else works very well, but my hands hold me up, lay me down, and I continue to fold them in prayer.

"These hands are the mark of where I've been and the ruggedness of my life. But more important, it will be these hands that God will reach out and take when He leads me home. And He won't care about where these hands have been or what they have done. What He will care about is to whom these hands belong and how much He loves these hands. And with these hands, He will lift me to His side, and there I will use these hands to touch the face of Christ."

I never saw the old man again, but I'll never forget what he said and will never think about my hands the same way. When my hands are hurt or sore or when I stroke the face of my children and wife, I will think of the man in the park. I have a feeling he has been stroked and caressed and held by the hands of God. I, too, want to touch the face of God and feel His hands upon my face—and I pray you do too.

Unknown Author

CHAPTER 50

Remember You Are God's Child

To those of us who are "senior saints,"
(Yes, I'm in that category, too!)
The years that we thought would be "golden."
Are like "brass" with all we go through.

Every day can bring a new struggle.
There can be more bad days than good.
But, remember, you are God's child.
And your feelings are well understood!

He promised He would never leave you,
And He's proven this time and again!
Don't give in to the song of "self-pity."
That starts when you feel "done in."

Don't let trials and fears assail you.
Lean on His Everlasting Arm!

This is when you must really trust Him
To keep you safe from harm.

God still has His plan and purpose
Which He does not want you to forget.
He loves you, and to Him, you're important.
He's not finished with you yet.

You can still share His love with others,
And pray God will draw those you love.
You are one of His "vessels of honor."
Which He chooses to use from above!

Rejoice, for God is still in control.
He's your Source and will meet every need.
Let the mind of Jesus be in you,
And you'll be blessed in each word and deed!

Robbie Mickley

CHAPTER 51

Write It Down

Getting older is anything but fun, but some of the things we do and say are really a hoot! This is especially true if our hearing and memory might be slightly diminished, then it's time to write it down...like this dear couple.

Write It Down

An eighty-year-old couple was worried because they kept forgetting things all the time. The doctor assured them there was nothing seriously wrong except old age and suggested they carry a notebook and write things down so they wouldn't forget.

Several days later, the old man got up to go to the kitchen. His wife said, "Dear, get me a bowl of ice cream while you're up." "Okay," he said..."And put some chocolate syrup on it and a few cherries, too," she added. "You better write all this down." "I won't forget!" he said.

Twenty minutes later, he came back into the room and handed his wife a plate of scrambled eggs and bacon. She glared at him. "Now, I told you to write it down! I knew you'd forget." "What did I forget?" he asked. She replied, "My toast!"

Unknown Author

PART II

Animal Stories and Other Tales

CHAPTER 52

Dusty: A Gift of Love

It was a cold rainy, miserable day, and I felt just like the weather. I went to work and sat down at my desk, and gazed out the window with tears brewing. I didn't feel like being there and swallowed the hard lump in my throat and said a prayer, "Dear Lord, before I look at the picture on my desk, help me overcome the pain in my heart."

In the stillness of that moment, the Scripture that came to me was "Behold, I shall make all things new." I quickly looked up the reference in my Bible and read:

And He shall wipe away every tear from their eyes; and there shall no longer be any death; there shall be no longer any mourning, or crying, or pain; the first things have passed away. "Behold, I am making all things new." And He said, Write, for these words are faithful and true.

Revelation 21:4-5

Here I am, a grown, mature woman (in fact, a senior citizen). Yet, when you lose something you love, age doesn't matter. Pain is pain. I felt like a broken-hearted kid who just lost his best friend—and I had.

I finally had the courage to look at the photo: I saw myself and a chestnut horse named Dusty. The picture was a "Kodak" moment caught on camera. With tears in my eyes and joy in my heart, I remembered the first time we met.

He was twelve years old, and I was in my late thirties. As I walked up to him, he looked at me curiously with his soft brown eyes. He was not the greatest horse I've ever seen, but he had a pretty face, and his amber eyes were unforgettable.

He had a beautiful chestnut coat that glistened like a shiny penny in the sun. A summer breeze tossed this flaxen mane and tail gently in the air, making an impression I will never forget.

He was big and tall and looked like a gentle giant. I giggled at the way he was standing because his front knees overlapped—like a kid that needs corrective shoes. As I held out my hand to say "Hello," I noticed the white diamond mark on his soft pink nose and the white hairs going all the way up his face, ending in a white blaze.

Buying a horse is a big decision and a lot of responsibility. My husband and I looked at him and went back home. A week later, we went back for a second look, and without me knowing it, my husband wrote a check to buy him. He came back waving a receipt and said, "His name is Dusty, and he's a gift of love."

So Dusty came home with us. We kept him at a local stable and quickly learned that he liked carrots more than apples. He had the most wonderful canter—smooth with long strides—and a fast trot that showed how well he moved. In fact, over time and with proper training, he became a champion dressage horse and jumper.

We had a wonderful trainer that took him from casual western riding to competition with the best of the best. Some people would snicker at him in the show circles—until they saw how graceful he was in the arena. He competed with horses that had generations of breeding and took home many First Place ribbons. The other horses were valued in the thousands, yet he was a divorce sale, with a skimpy tail and no horseshoes.

He had some bad habits in the beginning, but with steady training, we enjoyed our time together. Dusty loved to go on trail rides, jump, and take children for rides. We had so many good years together at the stables.

I remember lazy summer days riding bareback with the sun on my shoulders and a song in my heart. Or, I would just sit in a chair in front of his stall and eat an apple. The apples were for me since he preferred carrots. After he crunched on his carrots, he would stick his head over the rail and give me a horse kiss on the cheek.

When my parents grew older and needed more help, I had to cut down my hours at work to travel to their home some distance away on a regular basis. I had come to a crossroads and had to make one of the most difficult decisions of my life: to sell Dusty.

We had good offers, but I just couldn't sell him. When I talked to our trainer, she expressed interest if we could work out a price. The timing seemed perfect; she needed a lesson horse, and I need a home for Dusty.

Without hesitating, I said that he was far too valuable for me to price. I wanted to give him to her. Officially, Dusty was sold for one dollar and started a new career as a lesson horse. He went to work at a riding academy for handicapped individuals of all ages. Many adults rode him, and he was the favorite of the old and the young alike.

We were amazed when an eighty-year-old man rode Dusty in a horse show for the academy. Not only was that special, but the gentleman was blind! My husband and I attended the show, and we felt like proud parents sitting in the bleachers saying, "Hey, that's my kid." I was very happy that he was being used to touch so many lives.

As we were leaving the horse show, I stopped and looked back over my shoulder as he was being led away. He looked back at the same time and whinnied when he saw me. Our eyes met, and then he was on his way.

Just like the fork in the road, our lives had separated, but that was okay. The Lord was using him to help so many others in amazing ways.

Dusty went on to do private lessons after he left the riding academy, and I was able to visit him for many years. Just knowing he was there was a great comfort to me.

He lived to be thirty-one years old. His lasts days were spent out at pasture until he became injured and had to be put down. Although I had many years with him, there were never enough days. We shared our best years together, and though I chose to give him up, I have no regrets because he will forever be in my heart.

He was a gift of love, and because of these special memories, I can now look at the picture on my desk with more joy than pain.

CHAPTER 53

My Charly

The first time I ever saw Charly was when the kennel keeper at the animal shelter said, "Cute isn't he? If you'd like to see him, I'll be happy to open the cage. I sure hope he finds a home soon because tomorrow is his last day here."

The last thing I needed was to think about getting another dog, especially this one. He was a ragged-muffin-looking little mutt that had a cute face, bad breath, and shook when he was scared. He looked like he might be blond with dark-tipped ears, but his coat was so dingy it was hard to tell. He looked like a "Bengie" dog, but at this point, he reminded me of a rumpled tumbleweed.

My visit to the pound was not to get another pet, as I was mourning the loss of another dog. One rainy December evening, my husband and I came home to the horror of discovering that men working in our backyard left the gate open, and both dogs were gone.

One, we got back by a miracle, but the other dog was still gone, which led me to endless searching at the shelters. As I walked by all the locked cages, all the dogs perked their ears up at the sound of my footstep, but to no avail. All I could think about was finding my lost dog. That night I had the most unusual dream. I saw the face of that orphan dog at the pound, and it was so real. I knew I had to go back and get him the next morning.

As I walked down the vast isles of dog-death row, I flagged down the attendant and was relieved to see that the little vagabond was still there. As I leaned down to pet him, his eyes flickered with hope, but it was the fluttering of his tail that stole my heart. Joy filled my heart at the thought of saving his life.

The first order of business was to get him groomed. Ah, yes, he was blond and cleaned up beautifully. He was a mixture between a cockapoo and a mixed terrier and had the cutest face I've ever seen. We named him Charly just because it seemed to fit.

He was housebroken, loved kids, and was really smart. He spent the first few months hiding in the shrubs in the backyard but quickly came around with lots of love and attention. We took him on long walks, boat rides, and to the stables to see my horse. At bedtime, he would anxiously run up the stairs two at a time and settle himself on his floor rug, just to be by our side.

Sometimes a thunderstorm would send a spear of lightning flashing across the sky, shaking and rumbling everything, especially poor Charly. When this happened, with one might leap, he would spring from the floor to the bed and cuddle close until we all fell asleep together.

One night after work, my husband and I went out for a quick dinner and came home to a nightmare. Our house had been robbed! They came in through a sliding patio glass door in the backyard, but when the intruders left, they ran out the front door, leaving it wide open.

In the midst of all the confusion, we realized Charly was gone and had run out the front door, perhaps after the robbers. The police were called and were dismayed to see that our house was ransacked and all my jewelry was stolen, but that was not my concern. All I cared about was finding Charly, and we fervently prayed and asked the Lord to help us find him.

Our prayers were answered that night. A neighbor lady knocked on our door, and guess who she had tucked under her arms? We never recovered the lost jewelry, but I was ecstatic because my most valuable little jewel had been found...my Charly dog.

As the years rolled by, Charly got older too. He couldn't leap the stairs two at a time anymore and had stopped chasing cats, but he still slept on his rug, just to be by our side, as we carried him upstairs and say "goodnight."

Charly was with us for seventeen years, and as sad as it was to lose him, we are grateful for his life, his love, and the precious memories that will be forever in our hearts.

CHAPTER 54

Jack the Cat

Personally, I like dogs better than cats, but that was before I met Jack, the orange and white tabby that now rules our house. He was a "rescue cat," and you might say we redeemed his life from the pit. We first saw him at a pet center that had a section for rescued animals available for adoption.

He was about five months old, and we marveled at his beauty as he meandered over to see us through his cage door. He was caramel-colored but was mostly white and soft to the touch like a bunny. His tail looked like a taffy candy cane with perfect alternating colored stripes, and he had gentle eyes that were almond-shaped.

After serious thought, we went back to adopt him. We rummaged through the garage and found an old carry case, cleaned it up, and hurried back to the animal center to spring this pint-size tabby out of jail.

We finished filling out the adoption papers, and as we were standing in line to pay for everything, I couldn't help but think about God's redeeming love for us. Take a minute and think about it. When you rescue or buy a pet, you choose it, you purchase it, and now you're assuming the responsibility for its life. You are now committed to protect, provide and love the animal you have just redeemed. Now your pet has to depend on and trust you, the owner, to sustain its life. And you do it willingly out of love, not a forced duty, because it was your idea and plan.

If we do this much for a cat, just imagine how much more the Lord has done for us.

And so, our little redemption package came home with us. His name was Jack, and since he already knew his name, we didn't change it. However, it seemed like such a robust name for such a petite kitty. He weighed five pounds when we brought him home, and the first thing he did was run and hide under the bed.

As time passed and he grew up, we found him to be the most wonderful companion and lap cat. He loved to be petted and outgrew his timidity as a kitten. He was friendly with everyone, and only scratched on his cat post, and didn't destroy the furniture. Honestly, he didn't have any bad habits, except he's picky about his toys. He only likes the feather kind of things on a stick, and everything else is boring.

He certainly grew into his manly name, towing in at around sixteen pounds of muscular cat. He sleeps more as he's gotten older but still runs down the hallway like a speeding bullet and is still frisky. Sometimes when I'm getting ready in the morning and watching animal programs, he will sit on the bed and engage with the TV images. He especially likes the bird and fish variety of shows.

Not all cats are such wonderful companions, but he's the best one we've ever had. We call our big boy "Gentleman Jack" because he is a sweet, kind, and polite cat. One thing for sure, he loves his people, but if you come to visit, please leave your pooch at home because Gentleman Jack doesn't fancy any dogs in the house.

CHAPTER 55

Little Spud

It's no wonder they say man's best friend is a dog! It's easy to figure out why because dogs don't talk back, they're loyal and love you unconditionally. We've had many pets over the years, but little Spud deeply touched our hearts with his amazing desire to live and not die.

My husband and I planned a special vacation to celebrate our thirtieth anniversary. We didn't leave town often because of animal care, especially concerning Spud, but the animal clinic was familiar with his health issues and cranky disposition.

So we packed our bags, purchased our tickets, and went to Hawaii for a week.

On the third day of our vacation in Hawaii, I received an emergency call from the vet's office about our dog. Spud was having serious breathing problems, and his minor heart murmur was now a major issue with fluid around his heart. And, if this was not enough, there was a small cyst over his eye that burst, causing an emergency treatment.

We have never felt so helpless because we were so far away and had to make a decision about putting him down, or trying to rush home. Above all else, we didn't want him to suffer, but we also wanted to give him every chance. The thought of giving the vet approval to put him down over the phone was a heavyweight to carry, without a chance to be there to say goodbye.

We decided to wait on that final decision. The girls at the animal clinic took a special interest in him because they were amazed at this fight to stay alive. The reports were touch and go daily, as he clung to life with the hope of coming home. We prayed daily for him and knew God was in control, no matter what.

Just thinking about him brought back sweet memories of when he first came to live with us. He was on his way to the animal shelter because his previous family had to move and couldn't keep him. He was a Lhasa Apso mix and was a little dog with a big attitude...and a loud bark too.

Although he was a very loving little dog that liked to cuddle, we also learned that he had been abused and would bite if he didn't like something. I quickly learned this after cleaning his ears or brushing his tangled hair; I had to move really fast to avoid getting bit in the process.

He endured baths but hated water in his face, which took bathing to a new level of caution. When I took him for a walk, and a larger dog would confront him up close and personal, little Spud would stand his ground and not move an inch, and I smiled at his protective nature.

Previously, he had been given a really dumb name, which we knew had to be changed. However, one night the name issue was settled. He was cuddled next to my husband on the couch and snored so loud we had to turn up the TV. My husband casually said that he was a couch potato because of his sleeping and snoring, and thus the name "Spud" came about because he looked like a little white potato on the couch. Oh, great. Now I had two snoring machines at home!

Another memory we'll never forget was the time Spud got out of the backyard on the 4th of July. I was out of town, and my husband went with other family members to celebrate the evening. When he came home, the dog was gone and had dug under a fence out of fear when the fireworks went off. We had a very secure backyard with block fencing all around, but the side yard gate was wooden, and he found a way under it.

My husband was so upset he frantically searched the neighborhood until late that night. He finally gave up and went to bed around eleven p.m., but before his head hit the pillow, he whispered a heartfelt prayer to the Lord and asked Him to please help and send Spud home. At exactly that moment, the doorbell rang, and my husband stumbled to his feet in unbelief and went downstairs to answer the door. When he opened the door, he was shocked. It was an unknown neighbor a few blocks away with Spud on a leash.

She saw a dog running loose and was somehow able to catch him and brought him into her house until the fireworks were over. She thought he was a local pet and decided to walk him around the neighborhood, thinking he might remember his own driveway, and sure enough, he led her right up to our front door.

All these memories were with us the remaining days of our vacation until it was time to go home. Our flight was late that night, and we couldn't pick up Spud until the morning.

We were both apprehensive of what we would find as we waited in the lobby for the vet to talk to us. When they brought him out, he was thin and shaky, but just knowing we were there made his tail wag joyously. Even with his bad hearing and poor vision, he knew our voices. He snuggled his nose in my arms in a towel and looked up at me with his cute little button eyes, which said more than words can ever express.

We came home with a battery of pills, a big vet bill, but we came home with our little guy. He improved at home daily, gained back some weight, and still begged for snacks.

He still continued to snore on the couch and snap at me when it's bath time, but all in all, things were pretty much back to normal again.

He was a cranky little dog at times, but he trusted us in spite of his poor hearing and eyesight. We had him with us for quite a while after that, but after our last vacation, we decided not to take any more trips for a while.

What a lesson we learned from this little runt of a dog with a big attitude. By just hanging on to hope, he was able to cling to life and come home to those who loved him.

CHAPTER 56

A Song for Margo

Music is a wonderful way to overcome a bad mood or to refocus our minds on our favorite song. Sometimes the most majestic tunes are not those of acclaimed masters in symphonic halls but of the early morning serenade of the birds announcing the beginning of a new day.

People vary with different gifts and talents; some can sing, but most can't. But who would ever think that a little bird wouldn't be able to sing? They are born for such things, except a little bird named Margo, for all she could do was chirp.

A Song for Margo

Margo was a common little brown wren that lived in the countryside. She had a nice family of brothers and sisters, and all of them could sing but her. As she was growing up, a very mean old music teacher named Mrs. Taylor would drag her out in front of the class and put her ear to her chest and say, "Where is your voice? I can't hear it!"

"It's here," Margo strained to say, but all the old teacher could hear was a soft chirp. All the other students could carry a nice tune, but Margo had a faint voice and couldn't sing. When the other little birds of the country would get together to sing their songs of praise to God, all Margo could do was hum a few notes while the others in the glorious choir would sing for the Master. Oh, how Margo want to sing a song to God to tell Him how much she loved Him, but she was forced to be still and didn't understand why she was different.

All the other birds could sing and talk without any effort, but she struggled just to chirp. For the others, chirping and singing were as natural as breathing, but for Margo, she had to push every sound out from her tiny diaphragm just to make a sound. After chirping for any length of time, she gave up and didn't want to be around others and went back to her nest to think about things.

It was in this moment of silence and solitude that Margo heard the Master's voice telling her how much He loved her. He said that the songs in her heart were louder and more beautiful than all the other voices of the countryside.

Father God gently reminded her that worship is more than singing, but an attitude of the heart. He said it was because of His great love for her that He had chosen her for a very special assignment that only she could do.

He wanted someone with a beautiful heart to tell all His creatures, great and small, of His great love for them. Margo pondered all these things in her heart. How could this be that she could share the Master's love with others since she could not sing? "I know," she said. "I'll write letters to all the others in the country so they can hear God's voice on paper."

Father God said that many of His creatures sing and talk about Him but have no love in their heart and have become noisy gongs or clanging cymbals.

After many years, Margo is still writing letters with only a chirp, but that's okay. Many of the older birds who were sick and dying came to know Father God because of the song in Margo's heart as she put God's voice on paper.

Someday Margo's voice will be healed! But if not, she knows that when she goes to heaven, she will have a private audience with the Father, and all the creatures great and small will marvel at the golden sound of her voice as she sings praises to her Heavenly Father.

"I will praise God's name in song And glorify him with thanksgiving." (Psalm 69:30 NIV)

Bossy the Cow and Careless the Crow Series

This is a series of seven humorous musings, which is a take-off on being married for over forty years. These stories are filled with priceless humor, annoying habits, and precious moments that bond us together in our daily lives.

Since most of us seem to marry someone totally different than we are (which you'll soon discover), I'm sure you can easily relate to the rubs and humor of these silly creatures in their telltale adventures of life.

And who knows...you might even see yourself in these unforgettable barnyard characters, better known as Bossy the Cow and Careless the Crow.

CHAPTER 57

First Anniversary Memories

As many of you know, the first year of marriage can be the most challenging. This was especially true for Bossy the Cow because she quickly discovered that Careless the Crow snored too much and marched to his own drummer.

Bossy the Cow and Careless the Crow
First Anniversary Memories

It all started on their honeymoon cruise. The room was small, and his snores were loud. The neighbors in the next cabin pounded on the bedroom wall every time Careless would rip off a loud snort. Not only that, they blasted their radio all night in retaliation, making it a miserable experience for everyone on the Bahia deck. Poor Bossy thought she would die of no sleep and wondered what she had done by marrying this noisy crow.

Well, they lived through the cruise. Bossy had learned to poke him with her sharp elbows and roll him over time and time again. She also had him use other devices like the nose strips and throat spray. However, he was still loud, no matter what, and she could hear him vibrate even through her state-of-the-art earplugs.

When their first anniversary rolled around, Bossy put a lot of thought into finding the perfect gift for Careless. However, she was surprised, not in a good way, at the gift he had given her. Bossy was thinking in terms of something with sentimental value like perfume, clothing, or a token piece of jewelry. She was looking forward to a keepsake kind of gift, signifying the hallmark of their first year together.

To her chagrin, his idea of a personal gift was a ping-pong table. It made perfect sense to him, being such a practical creature. He knew Bossy loved the game and could whip almost any critter in town, including himself. A lovely gift, but not quite what the young bride had in mind. When he presented the gift to her, she didn't know if she was going to laugh or cry; so she did both, which totally confused the poor crow.

The next year was a little better when she received a six-quart stainless steel cooking pot, exactly like the one he saw in the window at the hardware store. But the redeeming factor was that it had a beautiful pink ribbon on top, which made all the difference. Another year it was a beautiful glass dish for the coffee table, which is full of potpourri, making the house smell good. But as time passed, Bossy learned to appreciate the love in his heart and not the glamour of the gifts, which became precious in her sight.

CHAPTER 58

Silver Anniversary

Here's a behind-the-scenes story about two barnyard friends that met many years ago and recently celebrated their Silver Wedding Anniversary.

It all started twenty-five years ago when Careless the Crow asked Bossy the Cow to marry him in the harvest fields near the farm. Despite their obvious differences, it's a love story of devotion and great friendship.

Silver Anniversary
Bossy the Cow and Careless the Crow

When Bossy the Cow first met Careless the Crow, he was the most handsome crow she had ever seen. He had beautiful black hair, sparkling eyes and taught others how to design their nests. He was well respected in the community for his teaching ability, abstract humor, and friendliness.

They met at a barnyard Christmas party, and Careless fell madly in love with the sleek and graceful Bossy.

Bossy was the barnyard secretary, and in her younger days, had been a fashion model. She had many suitors before but fell in love with the charming crow. Their many differences made their lives interesting and fun. So after a year of dating, Careless popped the big question, and Bossy said, "I do."

Many times when they were out with other friends, Careless chattered all the time about his nesting projects, like an old schoolmaster giving lessons. Rarely would anyone have a chance to talk, as Careless waved his wings as he told his interesting stories. Graciously, the guests just nodded politely and smiled at Bossy as the biscuits were passed around the table again.

Careless was a clutter rat. He had piles of junk all over his office and yellow post-it notes everywhere. He rarely threw anything out, including bad food. In fact, one time after Bossy made a fruit salad for lunch, Careless went through the trash and retrieved a spoiled peach in the garbage can.

Needless to say, Bossy had a fit. There also was the time Careless retrieved a rotten zucchini from the trash, which was the last straw! From this point on, Bossy began sneaking out trash to keep peace in the family and oversee healthy meal choices.

Careless was deaf in one ear, and Bossy hated loud noises and had sensitive hearing. Bossy grew up in a quiet family, while Careless grew up in a family that squabbled at meals.

Another source of frustration was about making plans, any kind of plans. Bossy liked to make plans in advance, and Careless never made a plan unless he bumped into one. His famous retort was, "Let's just see what happens." Well, so much for trying to make decisions together.

Her darling crow was also a sound sleeper. He had been known to fall asleep on a rock and not be stiff the next morning. However, Bossy was a light sleeper and liked her own nesting pillow. Bossy tried to watch TV with Careless, but he surfed the channels continually, falling asleep with the remote control firmly under his wing.

Soon thereafter, things changed. Bossy loved Careless, but there was still a void in her heart, and she felt lonely. It was at this time that Bossy heard about a Bible study in the barn that her friends told her about. They urged her to read the Bible for herself and said, "Seek Him with all your heart, and He will be found."

Suddenly, Bossy knew what was wrong. God was not a part of her life or their marriage. By hearing His voice and having her heart open to His Word, she knew what was missing. It was at that time she could see her own sin and selfishness. She ran back to tell Careless, and much to her surprise, he agreed to go to church with her, and they became united in their faith. Bossy and Careless learned that faith comes by hearing the Word of God and if God is for you, who can be against you?

Even though they're still an odd couple, God has made their rough roads smooth as they reminisced about their twenty-five years together. And no matter what their differences are, they are united in faith and have learned to praise God in the good times and trust Him in the bad ones.

As Bossy looked back over their life together, she wrote this poem for Careless. And after twenty-five years, you learn that love is more than a feeling but a commitment of the heart.

> You are my love
> You are my life,
> And twenty-five years later,
> I'm still your wife!
>
> We have more cheers
> Than tears in twenty-five years;
> And each new day, God takes
> The two of us, like lumps of clay,
>
> And molds us together
> To show us His ways.
> We have learned to forgive;

And seek His love in
Each gentle word.

To be kind to each other
And the best of friends,
Knowing someday our lives
Here will end.

Yes, twenty-five years with more joy
Than pain, but the best part is
Knowing what we've gained.

The love of the Father and promise
Of heaven, the salvation of our souls,
And gifts unspoken.

Love to you,

Bossy

Careless gave Bossy one of his half grins and kissed
her on top of the head after reading the poem. She could
tell that he was touched, and a tiny tear trickled down
his face as he was overcome with emotion saying, "Love
you too, old girl, and hopefully, we'll make it another
twenty-five years."

CHAPTER 59

The Rubs and Humor of Life

As you know, Careless and Bossy have learned over the years to laugh over their differences instead of fight over them. The truth is that Careless didn't change much, but Bossy had to so that these things wouldn't drive her nuts.

For example, when driving a car, Careless wouldn't put on his seat belt until they were in heavy traffic, and then it was with one hand on his coffee mug. When rounding a corner, he turned the wheel like a military maneuver making Bossy hang on for dear life.

And heaven forbid if there's a speed bump because he would tackle it full speed ahead. Ah, the joys of a nice drive. Actually, Careless is a good driver, that is until someone does something stupid on the road, and then he rants and raves without ceasing.

Bossy really admired the way Careless could read a map and follow directions. He can find about anything except his car. He always seems to forget where he parked and is famous for getting lost in a parking lot. The real challenge was when Careless tried shortcuts because he always got lost, and trust me, it was never shorter. Plus, you can be assured that he would never stop and ask for directions. Oh well, it must be a male DNA thing, right girls?

Careless can read maps well, but the problem is he still refers to the Thomas Brother's Map Guide of 1992 and insists nothing has changed. Somehow the driving thing has worked out over time. Careless gets us there, but Bossy finds the car...no problem!

Careless is hard of hearing, and trying to talk to him is almost impossible sometimes. After repeating herself three or four times, Bossy is now screaming. She has suggested learning sign language, but that idea fell on deaf ears. After many years of struggling with this, they both are finally learning to be more patient and kind to each other.

And then it's movie night. Careless shakes his popcorn real loud in the quiet parts and rattles his candy papers forever. Poor dear, he doesn't realize how disturbing this is to others, but the worst thing is when he whispers to Bossy, his voice is louder than he thinks, and people turn around. Then when he's done slurping his coke, he drops the cup straight down on the floor from his chair. Bang, it hits the ground!

But the classic was many years ago. It was an afternoon movie, and it was supposed to be exciting, according to the reviews. Bossy was enjoying the show immensely, but Careless had nodded off. He went to sleep in his chair and started snoring. People in the audience looked all around to see where the racket was coming from, and somebody called out, "Tell that guy to shut up."

Bossy was horrified and gave Careless a swift elbow in the side—and seriously considered leaving him in the theater asleep and going home. This was one of the better times they both laugh about now. In hindsight, they have surmised that the Lord must certainly have a sense of humor by putting them together to help each other. Bossy always claimed that Careless was so irritating that God was using him as a pumice stone to knock off her rough edges.

Careless is abstract, contemporary, and artistic. Bossy is traditional, organized, and focused. But blended together, they complement each other. Careless made a classic statement once when they were fussing with each other. He said, "Our life is like using oil and vinegar for a salad; when mixed together, they taste good!"

Yes, indeed! These two ingredients mixed together are good, but without being blended...not so good! Bossy never forgot these precious words of wisdom that her beloved shared with her in one of his more prophetic moments.

Yes, Indeed. The two shall become one!

CHAPTER 60

Driving Each Other Crazy

Bossy was a gal who like things in order, and Careless was definitely just the opposite. She even had the junk drawer in the kitchen organized. Careless, on the other hand, collected piles of clutter everywhere.

The scary place was his office. He had post-its all over his walls but never kept a calendar. Then when he had a misunderstanding about a business meeting, he would frantically claw through his piles of papers looking for a lost phone number, but to no avail. Bossy tried to help, but Careless had his own filing system and didn't want to get organized, so she learned to leave him alone, at least as far as his office was concerned.

Bossy's favorite time of the day was early morning. She loved to have her coffee and read the Bible. Ah, the quiet beauty of a peaceful morning. However, when Careless woke up and poured himself a cup of coffee, he would beat the side of his cup with a spoon loudly.

Ding, ding, bang, bang, bang, which almost became a tune. Well, so much for the quietness of the day.

If Careless didn't get enough attention while Bossy was reading, he would make a guttural sound in this throat, like a frog croaking, trying to be cute.

Cute did not work. This was more than annoying by any standard. Then he would look at Bossy over the top of his granny glasses and give her one of his charming smiles as he continued to make noises in his throat.

After his morning appearance at the breakfast table, he would take his coffee with him and meander down the hallway to take a shower. With each step, his coffee splashed like a tidal wave on the beautiful carpet as he rambled down the hallway, quite unaware of his trail of destruction.

His coffee slops irritated Bossy more than anything else in the world. Careless said he didn't realize it; ha, just another crow trick Bossy surmised. How could anyone not be aware of java splashing all over the place? And to make matters worse, the carpet had to be cleaned, not to mention the expense. Bossy just shook her head and realized someone must have had profound insight before giving Careless his name.

It took years for Bossy to overcome this irritation. But as time passed, it just wasn't worth getting upset over. So now, instead of flying into a rage, Bossy quietly grabs the carpet cleaner and works on the spots in the hallway as she grits her teeth and shakes her head, saying, "Let's face it, girls, we have to pick our battles wisely."

Well, so much for the carpet story, but it was always fun shopping with Careless if you could find him. He had a way of disappearing in the store. Sometimes Bossy had to call him on his cell phone because he wandered off (especially in Costco). The same was true if they met with a small group of friends, Careless would stroll off, and she lovingly had to refer to him as her "meandering vine" when friends asked her where he was.

At the end of the day and before their evening meal, they would always pray together. Careless said lovely prayers, but Bossy always had to add on her own P.S. request in case Careless forgot something.

Bossy and Careless had a rough beginning when they were first married but worked out their problems. Over the years, they both learned to enjoy each other and not to sweat the small stuff.

So dear friends, it's not how well you start out, but how you work it out! So work it out, learn to laugh about your differences more than you fight about them...and you might end up enjoying each other!

CHAPTER 61

For Better or Worst

Here's some valuable advice you should consider before getting married. In the wedding vows, for instance, it's the other part of the commitment we forget: "For better or worse."

Bossy learned that firsthand when Careless had to take care of her one year when she fell and hurt herself. All of a sudden, she couldn't bathe, wash her hair, or even fetch her own meals. But her beloved Careless rose to the occasion and was a hero to help.

The hard thing was to be patient and wait for Careless to do things at his own pace. Some days he didn't have time to help her shower. Sometimes he would fix a meal but leave the dishes in the sink to crust over. Bossy was helpless to get up and take care of things, but she eventually learned to chill out about the dishes, but she did worry about the ants that took advantage of the situation.

Her beloved crow was good to help her get dressed, but sometimes the colors and clothes didn't match. He had to climb the stairs so many times (because he could only think of one thing at a time), and it made him cranky. Usually, women are more organized and would plan to bring down several things at the same time, but that wasn't how Careless tackled the mission.

First, he brought down the shoes, next the blouse, next the pants, etc. All these were separate trips up and downstairs, and he grumbled with every step.

All of these things were minor, but what really bothered her was the dripping toilet upstairs, which was directly over her bedroom downstairs. It pinged all night. The plumbing lines were old, and when Careless flushed the john, it sounded like a waterfall gushing through the walls before the water shut off then; drip, drip, drip all night.

Bossy had to stay in the room downstairs because of her injuries and couldn't climb the stairs. The water drip was directly over her head in the makeshift bedroom downstairs. It sounded like the water was going to splat on her forehead at any minute.

She complained for weeks for Careless to fix it, but since he couldn't hear the dripping water, it never got done. Finally, a friend brought her a pair of earplugs, which helped immensely.

Careless had seen Bossy at her best and worst, as we all do when we've been together for a long time. Poor Careless had to do all the housekeeping chores, which

Bossy normally did. He also was working from his home office, which made extra work for him, but he was glad to help...most of the time.

Since Bossy was downstairs recuperating, and Careless was upstairs in his office, getting him to hear her suddenly became a problem. He couldn't hear her calls for help, so now she had to get creative. To solve the problem, Bossy found a bell with a ringer, and if she dinged it long enough, Careless could finally hear it.

It really didn't matter, it all worked out, but years later, Careless confessed he hated being beckoned by a bell to come hither on a rescue mission.

These kinds of trials bring out the best and worse in all of us. But the important thing to remember is that love is an action word, so do the right thing, even if you don't feel like it. God will honor your commitment and make your rough roads smooth, for better or worst.

CHAPTER 62

Forty Good Ones

In looking back at their life together on their fortieth anniversary, Bossy the Cow and Careless the Crow are reminded of 1 Corinthians 13, commonly referred to as the love chapter.

In hindsight, it's the irritating things that drove you nuts that are now laughable, as these memories are now precious and not deal-breakers.

Bossy quickly remembered all the nights that Careless would fall asleep on the couch with the TV remote huddled under his wing, which he guarded with his life. After several nudges to wake him up, he would growl like a bear when Bossy tried to get him up off the couch.

The next course of action was to get a stick and gently poke the sleeping grouch, who hollered if you woke him and complained worse if you left on the sofa. Unfortunately, Bossy was unable to roust Careless off the lumpy couch many evenings. So in the morning, he was stiff and sore, cranky to boot, but the worst part was his monster breath in the morning.

Bossy also cringed when she had to pick up his used toothpicks and discarded chewing gum he stuck on the coffee table magazines before he fell asleep on the couch; yuck, what a distasteful job. If she prevailed in getting her sleeping crow upstairs to bed, she had to make the rounds to be sure the house was locked and safe. Yes, the doors are locked, the lights out, and all is well.

One year Careless moved his business office in town to the bonus room at home. After years of hoarding boxes of paper from forty years ago, the bonus room became the "little" room post-haste. There was stuff crammed in every nook and cranny, which even Careless forgot about.

Finally, the move was complete. But even Careless had to admit he couldn't find things, and that was a scary statement! Careless had dozens of calendars but didn't use them. Instead, he relied on post-its stuck all over his overhead drafting light, which fell off as they aged and curled into an unknown pile.

Well, enough of tattling on Careless. Bossy has her share of annoying habits too. In fact, too many to mention in this letter, but through it all, Bossy and Careless thank the Lord for their forty good years together.

The key to survival in marriage is to give each other as much mercy and grace as God gives us. The key is to learn to forgive easily and be thankful. Let the other person know you love them in word and deed. Bossy then had the idea to write down some of the reasons why she loved Careless, which she gave him in his anniversary card. This touched the old boy's heart because he kept this love note in a very special pile in his office.

I Love You Because

I love your prayers that we share together every evening.

You are kind and willing to help others.

You love all our little animal friends.

You are a good provider, hard worker, and love your family.

You help me when I'm sick or need to go to the doctor.

You are my friend, my love, and partner in life.

You are friendly with all people and love to chat.

You are smart, handsome and interesting.

You like to get up early and are in a good mood.

You like to cook and clean up your mess.

You are good at your job and helpful to everyone.

You're my husband, and I'm grateful you're mine.

I love dancing with you...and your hugs are the best!

Your Bride,
Bossy

P.S. I don't want you to get too puffed up, so I'm going to let you feast on these words and say, "Happy Fortieth Anniversary" to my handsome, cute, and quirky husband.

I pray we will have many more years together and make each day count, and I found a special Scripture that talks about a journey of forty years too.

> The LORD your God has blessed you in all the work of your hands. He has watched over your journey through this vast wilderness. These forty years the LORD your God has been with you, and you have not lacked anything.
>
> Deuteronomy 2:7 (NIV)

CHAPTER 63

Ode to Retirement

Oh goodness, where do I start! All I can say is that retirement is not for the faint of heart. You would think after working all your life, getting along with your spouse would be a cakewalk...not exactly; it's more like a tightrope.

Careless was used to a quiet homestead with Bossy at work, and when she vacuumed early in the morning, he cringed and said she was noisy. Careless had been working at home a few years before Bossy retired, so all of a sudden, all their routines were different.

Bossy was used to time clocks, routines, and schedules. Careless, on the other hand, could read the paper in his robe and diddle on the computer all morning, plus he was not interested in eating breakfast most of the time.

Bossy, on the other hand, was used to eating early, so this eating schedule was up for grabs. But she continued to try and plan nutritional meals, but her beloved crow's idea of healthy food was hot dogs, cheese puffs, and a beer.

I know we've talked about driving before, but things change when you get old and retire. Bossy does most of the driving now, with Careless the co-pilot. This definitely was a new level of stress to deal with. She was not used to driving with a squawking crow, and he was anything but a silent old bird. He would not hush. He constantly chattered, saying, "Turn here, watch out for pedestrians, park here, oops, you missed your turn, and watch out," all in the same breath.

Poor Bossy, her head swiveled like an owl, trying to listen to him, check the mirrors, and focus on the serious business of operating a motor vehicle.

What was really hard was backing up in a parking lot. His head blocked her view until he finally agreed to sit still and not be so helpful. But to be absolutely fair, Careless saved the day more than once with his helpful hints. It took a while, but the driving thing is working out.

Another adjustment was seeing what Careless did during the day or didn't do. What never ceased to amaze Bossy was his perception of a quiet, restful day. This usually happened after Bossy took out the trash, went to the market, cleaned the house, swept the patios, did several loads of laundry, and cooked the dinner.

Careless did the dishes and never complained about helping. Yes, indeed a quiet, restful day for Careless as he played solitaire card games on the computer, why Bossy lay limp on the couch.

It has taken Bossy more than two years to power down after leaving her job of many years. Careless still works on a few architectural jobs at home. Bossy is amazed to watch the old master at work. She marvels at the knowledge and talent he has accumulated over the years at what he does best.

Bossy and Careless both like to read and love sitting on their patio in the warm weather. They also play games of Scrabble, in which Careless wins most of the time. These are two hobbies they can do together, but they have learned to give each other space for individual interests.

Careless seldom watches daytime TV, but watching the evening news is another story. Everything goes smoothly until he pushes the wrong button on the TV remote, and his program goes haywire. Then he yells loud and clear for Bossy to come and help. Same thing with the dishwasher; all those buttons are too much. And don't even ask about computer technology, especially for a guy who has one of the original flip cell phones.

It truly takes two of us to get anything done, especially at the doctor's office. I'm the driver and the ears. I also rat him out at the doctor's office, if necessary. Other than that, it's a nice outing if he doesn't try to drive from the passenger's seat.

Bossy and Careless prefer to call their retirement years their refurbishing years, which means to bring something back to a cleaner, brighter, or more functional state. And one of their favorite Scriptures is:

"But those who wait on the LORD shall renew their strength; they shall mount up with wings as eagles; they shall run, and not be weary, they will walk and not faint." (Isaiah 40:31 KJB)

Careless really likes this Scripture because of the bird fellowship he admires with his eagle friends.

Even though Bossy and Careless are challenged by the aging process, their faith and trust in the Lord are growing stronger every day, and they hope and pray the same will be true for you too.

P.S. Should you retire...have fun and don't fight!

PART III

Special People &
Family Letters and
Short Stories

CHAPTER 64

A Tribute to Raymond

I met an elderly gentleman years ago at a café on my lunch break from work. His name was Raymond, and this story is a tribute to his military service as a veteran and his faith in God in the last years of his life.

He sat all alone and never dressed well. Sometimes he shaved, but most of the time, he didn't. His smile was charming even though a couple of teeth were missing, but that didn't matter. I recognized his loneliness because of helping my dad for years, and we exchanged greetings whenever we saw each other in the restaurant.

Then one day, he asked me if I'd like to share his table for lunch (there was nothing else available), and we started chatting, and he talked about his life. I thought to myself; older people are so interesting; it's a shame people don't take time to talk to them.

He was a fighter pilot in World War II, and his age was hard to guess. Later I learned that he was over ninety and lived alone in the apartments across from the café. He went daily to the sandwich shop and sat for hours with a bowl of soup and coffee just to be around people.

I didn't see him for months because I was at home on a medical leave of absence from work. When I returned to my office, I wondered if the old man was still alive, then felt the urgency to talk to him about the Lord.

One day I drove by the café and saw Raymond sitting at his table, but I kept driving and ignored him. I found another place for lunch and ordered my meal.

As I was eating my lunch, I believe the Lord spoke to my heart and said, "Go back and talk to him; he's waiting for you." I had prayed about talking to him about God, but now I was running away from the challenge. I was afraid I wouldn't say the right thing or not have the courage and boldness to speak up.

In obedience to what I believe the Lord whispered in my heart, I went back to the café. When he saw me, he grinned and motioned for me to sit down. I hadn't seen him in months, and he looked frail and had aged considerably.

We struck up a conversation again, but this time he started talking about dying. Without hesitation, I looked him straight in the eye and said that we were all going to die, but asked if he ever thought about God?

He said, "No, not much because I was a military man, and it's too late for me." I said it was not too late! I told him as a military man, "You saw the horrors of war like my father did, and I thanked him for his service and sacrifice. It's because of men like you that fought for our country that we can live in a free nation."

I handed him a Gospel tract that I had tucked away in my purse in case I saw him. He read the Gospel tract at the table and said nothing but smiled at me lopsided. After a long time of silence, he said, "I don't know how to pray." I said, "Just talk to God like you're talking to a friend." I could see he was interested but didn't know where to start.

Then I gently said, "Raymond, if you want to, take my hand, and let's pray." His aged and spotted hand reached out for mine, and I said a simple prayer. He shut his eyes and held my hand tightly. After I was done, he gave my hand a little extra squeeze and said, "Thanks...guess that makes me official now." I said, "Yes, and all the angels in heaven are rejoicing over your prayer today!"

That Christmas, I bought him a Bible, and he said he would greatly treasure it and read it daily. A short time after that, he fell and had to go into a retirement home. I visited him once and learned a few months later that he passed away.

I will miss seeing Raymond at the café, but I'm so grateful that I had the opportunity to know him and was blessed by his friendship and life.

And as for Raymond, praise God he had the assurance of heaven before he died. And just like I told him in the café, someday we will rejoice together over that prayer at the lunch table...and all the angels will say, "Amen."

CHAPTER 65

My Friend MaryAnn

Some of my best memories in life are those of my working days and the special friendships I made over the years. I worked for a non-profit organization for over twenty-five years and met many wonderful people, especially a lady named MaryAnn. Not only were we co-workers, but we became special friends and soon discovered that we both shared the same doctor.

I'd seen MaryAnn for some time at work, but her office was across the street from mine. It was the same campus, but the company had several buildings to house all the employees, and we rarely saw people from the other locations.

One day I was at lunch with a girlfriend, and sitting across the aisle was MaryAnn. She was sharing lunch with someone else too. We smiled and said hello, but at that time, we only knew each other by sight. After we returned to work, MaryAnn called my office, and we talked for a few minutes about nothing in particular.

MaryAnn had a wonderful voice, and she was such an easy person to talk to. Then out of the blue, she asked if she could ask me a personal question; I shyly said, "okay."

Then she asked about my voice. My shoulders slumped, and my cheeks burned. She sweetly asked me not to be embarrassed because she recognized the neurological condition causing my strained voice at times. Then she told me about her struggles with Parkinson's Disease, and before you knew it, our friendship bloomed. We also discovered we were seeing the same doctor for neurological disorders. We now had more in common than ever and constantly encouraged each other with our challenges.

One of the last things MaryAnn shared with me before her health declined was this beautiful poem:

> I see you standing tall,
> Like a pillar of light and beauty;
> A garland of Grace is on your head.
> You are rich in the glory
> Of God's unlimited resources.
> You are a carrier of the blessed light.
> God has called you to be as a burning sun in
> His Kingdom, shining brightly, boldly, and a
> joy to those whose lives you touch.
> I'm so glad you are in my circle of love.
>
> Unknown Author

As time went by, she had to retire because her disease progressed with Parkinson's. She stopped seeing my doctor and found someone else to help her.

She never returned to my physician, but each time I saw my doctor for my throat injections for Vocal Cord Dysphonia, he asked about her. He was the head of a neurological institute and expressed his concern that her current medication was not well suited for her.

The years went by, and she became worse. The latest note I had from her family was that she was bedridden and hospitalized. My doctor was deeply grieved to hear about her condition and asked me to call her family and extend his offer to help, once again.

I really didn't want to get involved with this but felt burdened to call her family, as the doctor asked. I prayed and got others to pray too. The family was very gracious and thanked me for my concern, but related they were not interested. I was disappointed but understood completely.

But in my heart, I knew that God wanted to use this doctor to help MaryAnn. However, the next day everything changed. I received a call from her family, and they had a complete change of heart. They wanted my doctor to see her ASAP at the hospital because she was unable to travel.

My doctor was good for his word and made arrangements to see her at another facility. I helped coordinate a meeting with her family and my doctor at the hospital.

I waited for the doctor in the parking lot, knowing how hard it might be to connect all parties and make this work out smoothly. It was a big medical center, and suddenly I started to panic. What if the doctor gets lost or doesn't show up?

Oh dear, God! I must be nuts for doing this, and I wasn't sure if I should stay in my car or wait inside because there were several lobby locations. As the clock ticked away, I decided to stay put, but it was the middle of summer, and I was sweltering in my car waiting for the good doctor.

I said a quick prayer. As I waited anxiously in my automobile, the Lord spoke to my heart and said I would hear in eighteen minutes. Now that's a specific answer to prayer, even though I had my doubts, but in exactly eighteen minutes, my cell phone rang, and it was the doctor. He called me as he pulled into the driveway, and I could see him from where I sat in the parking lot. The doctor and I walked to MaryAnn's room, where the family was gathered. I was so excited to see everyone I overlooked her condition, but my doctor stopped dead in his tracks.

Without saying a word, he began his evaluation, but I could tell that he was dismayed at her physical condition. In spite of her declining health, her face was still beautiful with pretty heart-shaped lips, and her eyes sparkled through the pain when she saw me. The doctor took over her case on a temporary basis, and there were positive improvements. I went to see her the following week and noticed that her speech was clearer and her shaking was better too.

I noticed a Bible on the table next to her, which she had friends and family read to her at every opportunity. She was released from the hospital a short time later and sent home with a caregiver. She had a loving family to support and comfort her, but the best part was watching God work behind the scenes to help people and answer prayers.

God does miracles every day!

CHAPTER 66

A Prisoner of His Love

In the Introduction of this book, I gave a brief explanation of how these letters began. Originally, they were sent out to individuals, retirement homes, and to a local prison in northern California.

Over the years, one of the most precious gifts I've ever received was a handmade card sent by a group of inmates in prison. These men individually signed short notes of encouragement saying how much the letters blessed them, and they, in turn, passed them on to their families.

I was so overwhelmed with the labor and love put into this handmade card sent to me through my approved contact at this facility that I wanted to do something special for them, but what?

After much thought, I labored most of one weekend and wrote a poem just for them, and I believed it came from the Father's heart, and I named it: A Prisoner of

His Love. These men are confined in their lifestyle, but they were free men in Christ, and prisoners of His love, which knows no limits or boundaries.

A Prisoner of His Love

I see the brokenhearted and the loss
I see the lonely and its cost.
I see the need great and small
To answer My loving call.

Will you let Me take off those chains?
Will you give up those gangs?
Will you stop playing the "blame games"
And let My love erase their false claims?

I'm with you in that cell,
Come to Me and feast and dwell.
I gave you my Word and My Son
Reach out for me and take My hand,
And I'll take you to the Promised Land.

I love you more than you will know,
I love you more than I can show.
Receive by faith My sacrificial heart,
That died for you to give you a start.

You're safe in My hand,
And your life is Mine to command.
But are you willing to stand
For what I ask in this hostile land?

 I want your love and your heart
I always did, right from the start.
It was not My plan for evil to reign,
So I sent My Son to die in pain.

And by His precious blood is your gain
To live a life free from stain.
He died to set the captives free
That faithful day at Calvary.

To bring a blow to Satan's bow
So that truly you will know.
I am the way, the truth, and the life.
Why continue to live in strife
Killing each other with a knife?

What more can I do to show you the way,
And keep you safe throughout the day.
Will you let My love set you free,
And keep you ever close to Me?

I will walk with you and talk with you
And give you strength when you have none.
I will fill you and heal you and make you My own,
And be the Father you've never known.

Janeen Stoffregen

My Story

I'm including a letter I wrote many years ago to a pastor that I never met but listened to on the car radio (quite by accident) on my way to work.

Listing to this program became the beginning of a life-changing experience for me, and little did I know as I wrote this simple letter that it became known as "my testimony." I had no idea what that meant, only that the Lord had changed our lives and healed our marriage.

With no further expectations of hearing anything about my letter, I was shocked weeks later when I received a letter from the pastor, asking permission to share my story with his church. I was totally astounded, and after my husband and I discussed it, we agreed to his request, hoping it would help other people.

We were invited down to the pastor's church the day he planned to read my letter live to his audience. However, he was called away at the last minute for an emergency, but we were warmly welcomed by his staff.

My letter was not shared that day but was read at a later date. Some years later, I met the pastor personally.

He was teaching at a local church in our area, and we had an opportunity to talk with him. He still remembered my letter and said there were lots of responses. We hugged and greeted each other like long-lost friends and marveled at the mysterious ways that God works.

Dear Pastor,

Please find enclosed a small donation that I would like to make to your church. I have never been to your church, but your message one night reached me on the car radio.

While driving home from work, I listened to you on a local radio station, and your words sunk deep into my thoughts. Actually, it seemed to be a message personally directed to me. I was not a believer at the time, nor did I listen to Christian anything. The car radio had been pre-set with stations, and I was simply flipping buttons in search of something different.

The message that night was about blaming your family, friends, or parents for your unhappiness and letting go of the hurt and disappointment others have caused you. You kept saying, "Read your Bible, it will change your life." Boy, that is the truth!

My husband and I had been married for about ten years when everything fell apart. He was a backslider (which he called himself), and I didn't know the Lord, had no interest in church, and seldom thought about God. I was never married before, nor did I have any children. After getting married, I became a stepmother to a fifteen-year-old girl (that lived with us) and an eleven-year-old boy that was there mostly on the weekends. We had had anxiety and strife in every aspect of our "blended life" for many years. As if this wasn't enough to bring me to my knees for help, the real breaking point happened years later when we tried to adopt a baby since we couldn't have our own children.

My husband canceled the adoption days before the final arrangements were made. I found that family (on both sides), friends, and relatives simply didn't want anything to do with this situation and were not supportive, even from the beginning. I carried all the bitterness of betrayal, anger, and resentment with me for years, as nobody wanted to talk about the adoption that died; it was never discussed again.

My anger was directed at everyone; my husband, parents, family, and even my employers.

Finally, I was broken. I was numb both emotionally and physically and cried out to God to help me—and He did. Shortly after hearing you on the radio, I became more interested in knowing about the Lord and purchased my first Bible and started a new journey.

I also found a local Bible-believing church and went by myself for a while, but then my husband joined me. Shortly after that were baptized together and share our faith continually with each other.

The Lord had another plan for me because after I became a believer, I started working for Christian ministry and truly loved my work. I learned how to forgive people that hurt me realized that I could be fulfilled completely without having a child of my own.

I love your program. God is using you in a special way to reach others, not only in your area but for all your radio audience too. Keep up the great teaching and preaching, and I'll catch you on the radio.

CHAPTER 68

Letter to My Parents

After my husband and I came to faith in Christ, we entered into a whole new world. Many of our friends and family members didn't understand our new exuberance about going to church, reading the Bible, and growing in our faith.

However, we both loved our families and many times tried to share our faith with our loved ones. My family, in particular, was especially difficult. My mother was a wonderful person but deeply influenced by a New Age religion, and obviously, there was a clash between our views and beliefs in these things.

My dad was a very stoic person and wanted nothing to do with organized religion of any kind. Although I had wonderful parents, church was not a part of our family life growing up. As time marched on, I was deeply concerned about their faith in God, especially after they had a near-fatal car accident that almost took their lives.

In order to reach out to my parents about the Good News of the Gospel, I found conversations to be useless, so I resorted to writing them a letter. I'm glad I had the courage to approach my parents because they finally came to faith in Christ before they died!

Dear Mom and Dad,

This is a letter to you both that I am writing in complete love, kindness, and gratitude to you as my parents. In our lifetime, we seldom take the time to say just how much we love each other, even though it's always assumed and quietly understood.

I realized how close I came to losing you both in that terrible car accident you were in, and then it would be too late to tell you all these things.

If you and Dad had died, and thank God you didn't, could you be sure you'd both go to heaven? Things like this are hard to talk about because many of us believe if we're good people and think of others and do nice things, we will go to Heaven automatically.

We all feel we can do it "our way," and there are many roads to Heaven, but we are judging our life and actions on our own standards, not God's.

The truth is that being a good person or always doing nice things is wonderful, but you can't earn your way to Heaven with all your good works. Jesus is more than just a good teacher; He is the bridge between God (being holy) and man (being sinful).

Jesus said, "I am the way, the truth, and life: no man cometh unto the Father but by me" (John 14:6).

I'm writing this letter because it seemed like the best way to reach you both and share with you what I know in my heart. Like so many other families, we didn't talk much about God or religion and have only gone to church a few times together.

This is not about religion, church traditions, positive thinking, or admiration of creation. This is about life and choosing your eternal destiny forever.

This is about knowing the living God and having a personal relationship with Jesus. To know God, you must believe that Jesus was the Son of God and that He died on the cross for our sins and rose from the dead on the third day, proving that He was God's Son! He conquered death for all of us that believe in Him. He paid the price for our sins, past, present, and future, with the shedding of His blood.

Many people are confused about what sin is and feel if they have not stolen, robbed, killed, or done something really terrible, they have not sinned. On the contrary, sin is many things, but the Bible says pride and self-righteousness will deceive many un-believing people.

The Bible also says, "for all have sinned and fall short of the glory of God" (Romans 3:23). God knows it's impossible for us to keep His standards, and that's why He sent His Son as the ultimate sacrifice to purchase our salvation by His death on the cross.

The most important thing to remember is that we are saved by our faith in Christ, not our works. For by grace you have been saved through faith; and that not of yourselves, it is the gift of God.

Ephesians 3:8

If you want to know Jesus in a personal way, all you have to do is sincerely pray from your heart and invite Him into your life, admit you've made mistakes, and ask for forgiveness. If you truly mean this, you will see changes in your life and your at-titude. This is what happened to us, and you've seen how God has changed our lives and healed our marriage, as you've mentioned before.

This is the most difficult letter I have ever sent you, my dear parents, so please let these words sink *deep in your heart and know I love you enough to tell you the truth.*

There are so many wonderful things to look forward to in Heaven, and one of the most comforting will be that we will see our loved ones again. Once we pass through this life to the next one, we will know our friends and family there. I want more than anything to know that someday I'll see you and Dad there, and we'll all be together again.

Love you both,

Janeen

CHAPTER 69

Dad's Seventy-Fifth Birthday

My mother was my go-to person. She and I had weekly conversations, while my dad remained his stoic self year after year. I loved my dad, but he was not much of a communicator with anyone, and as a daughter, I greatly missed having a close relationship with my father.

On his seventy-fifth birthday, I decided to live on the edge and send him a personal letter. A week later, I drove out to their house to celebrate Dad's birthday with a few other family members.

When it was time to line up for a few photos, I was standing next to Dad, and with a sudden nudge of his elbow, he leaned over and said, "I liked your birthday letter."

I was shocked that he told me, but so happy! My father was a man of few words, so for him to acknowledge the letter was a big deal, and I'll never forget it.

Dear Dad,

In honor of your seventy-fifth birthday today, I wanted to give you a special gift that will last longer than a new shirt or a gift pack of your favorite sausage and cheese.

I wanted to share with you some of my favorite memories about you as I was growing up. I thought this might be a good idea since it has never been easy for us to share our feeling as father and daughter.

I remember when I was little how you dressed up as Santa Clause and gave everyone gifts under the tree. This was a special Christmas because you brought home "Ginger," the hyperactive puppy that chewed her way through our house.

Another time I remember you gave me a set of plastic Appaloosa horses as a birthday present, which I still have and cherish today. You have always known how much I love horses ever since that first time you and Mom put me on a pony ride at Griffith Park.

I remember when we moved to the country and how you and Mom made a dream come true for a thirteen-year-old girl to own her own horse. I also remember how hard we worked in the hot sun painting the coral fence. Then there were all those times you fed the horse for me before school when the weather was bad, thank you! So many memories are special about you both. Like the times when I was hurt or in the hospital, and you and Mom were always there to show your love and care.

I'm not sure why we've never been close when it comes to talking to each other or showing outward affection. Maybe it's because we're shy or afraid to show our feelings.

The older we get, the harder it is to respond to our hearts because we have buried and ignored our feelings for so long. If a picture is worth a thousand words, then what do you think a hug is worth? I think it's worth more than words can ever say.

As long as you're alive, it's never too late to take that first step toward doing something that's on your heart. I know you want to reach out but don't know how to take the first step. I know how you feel because I didn't know how to unlock the closed doors of my heart either.

Oh, Dad, my heart is open now; it's nothing that I could have ever done by myself, not even with the best of intentions, hard work, or good deeds.

I was changed by the power and grace of God, reaching down and touching my heart, melting away all my bitterness with His tenderness and love.

Reach out, Daddy, and be willing to let Jesus embrace you on your seventy-fifth birthday, and know that He is the only One who can unfold the tightest of crossed arms and the hardest of hearts. Take that first step and reach out, and He'll be there to show you the way, the truth, and the life.

Birthdays are such special times. I hope we can share many more together. I think the best ones are yet to come, and I look forward to making new and special memories with you.

Love you,

Janeen

CHAPTER 70

Fear Not

"For I am the LORD your God who takes hold of your right hand and says to you: 'Do not fear; I will help you.'" (Isaiah 41:13 NIV)

After my mother was diagnosed with cancer, everything changed in my life as I entered into a new season of helping my elderly parents in their last days. But one weekend, after an especially stressful visit, my husband and I decided to do something fun and went to Disneyland.

It was a warm day, and after walking around for a while, we stopped to rest at an outside café. While hubby was getting us some soft drinks, I waited for him on the patio at a wobbly wrought iron table with chairs. The table was next to a walkway pavilion surrounded by a neatly trimmed hedge.

It was a great spot to rest in the shade and watch people. As I was waiting for my husband to return, I heard a bird frantically chirping nearby. I looked down into the hedge and could see he was trapped in branches. Instantly, upon seeing his condition, a surge of anxiety rose up within me; I, too, was surrounded by a formidable hedge of family problems with no way out.

But somehow, seeing this bird entrapped intrigued me as I wondered how he would get free, thinking, if there's hope for him, all the more so for me.

At that precise moment, I felt like the Lord was speaking to my heart through this word picture lesson by impressing these thoughts on my heart:

"I see you in the thicket of problems with your family, and My eye is on you, as your eye is on the sparrow. I will lead and guide you; fear not. I am watching over you. I see and hear your cries for help. I go before you always and will never leave or forsake you."

Tears welled up in my eyes. Here was this fragile little bird trapped in the hedge and unable to find its way out, yet God was in control and heard his chirps for help. My mind knew these things, yet my heart was fearful. Then an amazing thing happened right before my eyes. The little bird suddenly found its way out of the tangled maze of the wooded thicket and inched its way to freedom and joyfully flew away.

All of this took place in only a few minutes, and before I knew it, I was humming the song, "His Eye is on the Sparrow," and I know He watches over me.

CHAPTER 71

Homeward Bound

Before my mother passed away, I was able to talk to her about the Lord. Instead of bringing a Bible into her room, I memorized Romans 10:9 and talked to her about what that Scripture meant. She looked me in the eye and nodded her head slowly up and down that she understood and believed!

Tears of joy filled my eyes as I held her hand. I know she wanted to say this, but she couldn't. "Don't worry, daughter, your prayers have been answered." I could see that she was tired, so I let her rest. That was the last time I saw her alive. She died while we were eating dinner in the other room, shortly after I was with her.

A few days after Mom's funeral, my friend wrote this amazing Homeward Bound story and gave it to me. Not only did it confirm my mother's faith, but it encouraged mine as well. Her heartwarming story gave me a glimpse into the celestial portals of what my mother may have experienced as she took her first breath on the heavenly shores.

Dear Janeen,

The more that I pray for you, the more the Holy Spirit nudges me to write this and tell you that your mother is safe in the arms of Jesus. I want to mentally and emotionally walk you through what may have happened when your mother went Home.

Homeward Bound

Mother was in much pain and confusion. She kept going in and out of reality, it seemed, and she knew her daughter and her husband were there. She could not remember what day it was, and she was scared because she no longer had control over any of her body functions. She felt death was near, and oh, how she wanted peace.

She heard Janeen talking to her about Jesus again. Her mind wanted to reject it all, but something deep inside her caused her to know that her daughter was right. She had been watching Christian TV shows long enough to hear the same things her daughter kept telling her, in making her heart right with God.

It all was so foreign to all she had been taught, yet she could not help but see the great changes in

Janeen's life and her marriage. She knew she really had something she wanted.

What was it Janeen was saying now? That if she confessed that Jesus was God's Son and believed in her heart that Jesus died for her and God raised Him from the dead, she could be saved, as her daughter called it.

Well, that seemed so very simple; she could do that. Oh, she hoped Janeen knew she meant it when she asked her if she had done that. All she could do was faintly nod her head to say yes, and when she did, all of a sudden, she was flooded with peace! Great peace! Joyous peace! Wonderful peace!

All of her fear of dying was gone! She wasn't sure about all that was happening to her, but it wasn't long until her body felt so light, and it seemed she was being pulled upward. Where was she going? It was dark all around her, but she was being carried to this Light that was ahead of her, and almost immediately, it seemed like she was standing before a threshold.

She could hardly look in for the brightness of the Light. It was then; she felt a hand taking hers. For the first time, she felt shy about what might come next. She had always been in control, but this was very different. Everything was entirely out of her hands. So, cautiously, she allowed the hand to draw her into the Light.

Immediately, she gasped in awe and wonder at the beauty all around her. But, before she could really focus on that, she was drawn to look into the face of the One whose hand held hers. A beautiful smile illuminated His face and His eyes...Oh, she had never seen eyes like His! She felt like she was looking into deep pools of Love. And, as He looked upon her, she could feel herself being enveloped by that Love. She had never know Love like this. And, she knew it was for her.

Could this be Jesus, the One she had rejected for so long? She bowed her head, but He reached out with His hand, placed it under her chin, and drew her gaze back to His own. It was then she saw the nail prints in His hands. Oh, this was Jesus.

And, all that her daughter had tried to tell her must be true, that Jesus died for each person, and now she understood that He had died for her! "Yes, dear one. I am Jesus, and I loved you so much, I died for you. But, My Father also raised Me back to life again, so that once you simply believed in Me, you would be able to live with Me in My Father's kingdom forever."

"How delighted I am that you have accepted Me, and how much there is for you to learn. You *will be schooled here, but not until you have been shown the place I have prepared for you. I have angel attendants who will take you under their wings and teach you the ways of your eternal Home. Then, once you are ready, you will be schooled in that which you did not learn upon the earth. "*

"I can tell that you are overwhelmed with the facts that all this is real, so My angel attendants are coming to take you to the 'Welcoming House' for those who have just arrived. How pleased we are that you believed and will be with us forever." Mother was still speechless. There was nothing she could think of to say, except a quiet, "Thank You."

Jesus then gently hugged her and told her how much He loved her. He went on to say, "Your daughter has prayed much for this to happen, and her prayers have been answered. Now, she can joyously look forward to seeing you again, knowing you will never be parted but will live together in My presence.

"And, you will be waiting for the day when she, too, will be welcomed into her eternal Home. She now has a personal investment in the Father's Kingdom, and she can rest in My love knowing that you are here with Me." Just then, two shinning angels joined them. Jesus introduced them, and Mother felt very comfortable with them.

An excitement began to rise up within her. To think of what she almost missed and how glad she was that she had believed. Jesus assured her that she would see Him often and that they would enjoy precious fellowship together. And, she really wanted to get to know Him better!

He waved, and He went off to welcome another Home, and Mother went off with her angel attendants like a little child about to receive a surprise. She even felt like a little child as caring attendants led her to the "Welcoming House," from which she could hear joyous laughter and music. Oh, how glad she was that she had made her heart right with God!

I pray these words will lessen your grief, uplift your spirit, encourage your heart, and empower you with the strength of the Holy Spirit within.

Robbie Mickley

CHAPTER 72

The Last Present

It was the first Christmas present under the tree and the last one to be opened. In fact, it set by itself on the cedar chest at the foot of my bed for a long time. The present was carefully wrapped in a joyous holiday print, and the name tag was written by the shaky hand of my beautiful mother.

I couldn't bear to open the present. I wanted it to remain as a lasting legacy because there wouldn't be any more birthday cards, or Saturday morning chats, or Christmas presents under the tree since Mom passed away on Thanksgiving Day.

But before she became too ill, she ordered a gift for me in advance and had it all wrapped and ready to go. Weeks before Christmas, Dad went to the closet and retrieved the present she bought. It was carefully wrapped, and he handed it to me with a lonely tear running down his cheek.

I took the gift, and my lip quivered as I silently prayed that whatever it was, it would last a long time. I couldn't bear to open it then; it was too sad. I wanted it to last and knew it was the last present I'd ever get from Mom. I wanted to savor it, so I took it home with me. It made me feel like Mom was still here.

Finally, on New Year's Day, I mustered up the courage to open the present, and I was surprised to find the kind of gift my mother had never given before.

It was a set of tapes on the Bible, and I knew this was her way of letting me know she had faith in God and for me not to worry because she was with Jesus.

Yes, indeed, her last present will last forever! Even though the tapes will wear out, God's Word never will! It was a special gift in another way too, because it was the first time we shared our faith together.

"The grass withers and the flowers fade, but the word of our God stands forever." (Isaiah 40:8 NLT)

CHAPTER 73

Keep Looking Up

What better place to wrap up these Letters of Encouragement than with the hope of heaven! After all the difficulties, hardships, and challenges in life, we can confidently say that the Lord has helped us so far.

So fear not, weary traveler, because He is lovingly and carefully watching over you today! And when we take our last breath on earth and crossover into the threshold of Heaven, Jesus will be waiting for you. But in the meantime, here are some encouraging thoughts for you. So close your eyes, calm your mind and imagine Jesus cheering you on with these words:

"I know all the things you do. I have seen your hard work and patient endurance" (Revelation 2:2-9 NLT).

"You have patiently suffered for Me without quitting" (Revelation 2:3 NLT).

"I know all the things you do. I have seen your love, your faith, your service, and your patient endurance. And I can see your constant improvement in all these things" (Revelation 2:19 NLT).

The Lord sees our progress while we often focus on our failures, shame, and worries about the future. Thank God for His grace and mercy daily as He looks past our flaws and sees our needs.

So rise up, cheer up, and remember how much He loves you...and keep looking up!

God is with you!

Backstory

Like many of you, I have been confined at home because of the COVID-19 virus and taking preventative measures about healthcare safety, especially for my husband and myself as senior citizens. Yet, with this shut down of "business as usual" it's helped me to focus on putting this project together, and I'm grateful that I could redeem the time in such a constructive way.

My husband has also retired a short time ago from his architectural business, and while we have had our share of health issues, we are enjoying our time together and trusting the Lord one day at a time.

Other published work:

The horse story I shared in this collection was published in Today's Horse Trader magazine in October of 2006.

Snapdragon, a father-daughter story, was published by Westbow Press in 2013, under my pseudonym name of Allison St. James. This story captures the real-life drama between a loving daughter and her strong-willed father after her mother's death. She shares both humor and heartbreaking events of his final years. You'll be astonished by the difficulties, yet amazed by the answered prayers...a real faith-building story!

Snapdragon

A father-daughter story

Allison St. James

About the Author

Janeen Stoffregen lives in South Orange County, California, with her husband, Bill. They have two adult kids and four beautiful grandchildren (she's a stepmother) and had the joy of watching them grow up to be the most amazing, wonderful people.

CPSIA information can be obtained
at www.ICGtesting.com
Printed in the USA
BVHW041125060721
611236BV00017B/508